Nothing Matters . . .
but Delicious

Nothing Matters . . . but Delicious

A RADICALLY HONEST COOKBOOK

Greg Baxtrom

AND JOSHUA DAVID STEIN

Photographs by Murray Hall

TEN SPEED PRESS
California | New York

Staples

SPICES

CONDIMENTS

Salads

Soups & Stews

Snacks

Veggies

CONTENTS

Poultry

Meats

Fish

Carbs

Sweet Things

Drinks

ATHLETIC
BREWING Co.
COMICS
CLOPEDIA

I've lived my adult life in two unequal parts. But both are equally important to understand who I am, what this book is about, why I wrote it the way I did, and why it can be helpful to you. First chef; then alcoholic.

For the first thirty-four years of Gregory Millard Baxtrom, all I wanted was to be a chef. Not just a run-of-the-mill chef, but one of the greatest chefs in the world. I was a greyhound chasing a rabbit. Single-minded, fast, and panting. I wanted my face in the Mount Rushmore of the gastronomic world, beside Carême and Keller, between Bocuse and Boulud. Life was a flat-out sprint to culinary achievement, a grind for which I had been conditioned since birth.

I grew up in a rural farming community outside Chicago called Frankfort. It was a small town: a main street with a granary on one end, a real Midwestern dive bar with a blinking neon light, and a music shop with dusty guitars in the window. The town was small but the farms were huge, vast fields of corn that surrounded the five-acre plot where my family lived. My parents—Patti Ann and Mike—were quiet but tough Chicago people from the South Side. Mom was a schoolteacher; Dad worked his way up from cleaning restaurants at night to becoming a successful carpenter. He lived by a simple motto: "Do a job big or small; do it right or not at all," a couplet that I've adopted and taken to heart throughout my life.

Our family, though loving, was not one for half measures, not a cradle of quitting or a soft foam pit of "Well, I tried." Self-reliance, perseverance, and toughness were the Baxtrom family heirlooms, passed down to me, my older sister, Katie, and my younger brother, Kevin. Autumns raking. Winters shoveling snow. Summers chopping wood. Spring weeding. The Baxtrom stance, like many of our farmer neighbors, was head down and hands in motion. We didn't complain. We didn't object. We never quit. I, who was named after my dad's brother who had passed away after a car accident at only twenty-two years old, felt I had a special obligation to be the golden child. I was a Boy Scout, literally—do it right or not at all—then an Eagle Scout, for all Frankfort to see, in my blue neckerchief, vowing, on my honor to do my best, to do my duty, to God and my country.

Since Mom and Dad worked late and we kids—all tall—ran cross-country, dinner was a communal effort that was dispersed among the family. Whoever came home first started something, and whoever could finished it. We all ate together around our small wooden table. Even as a seven- or eight-year-old tasked with making popcorn for movie night, I had an aptitude for cooking. From popcorn I graduated to frozen Salisbury steak, then grilled chicken, then pasta. When I got my first job the day I turned fifteen, it was behind the fry station at the local Wendy's. No, I didn't vow to devote my life to the pursuit of Michelin stars over saucy nuggets on the weekend shift. But at Wendy's, the inner workings of a professional kitchen first fascinated me. I loved the rapidity of the orders in and out; was hypnotized by the monotony of dropping a basket of fries into a vat of oil; loved that, all things being equal and the menu never changing, you could still try to make the best fried chicken sandwiches you could. That was my job, small as it was, and I wanted to do it right.

INTRODUCTION

When I graduated high school, I headed off to Kendall College, a culinary and hospitality management school in Chicago. There, perhaps as a legacy of Scouts learning, I found I picked up techniques quickly. Personally, I found that in the rigor of a kitchen, with the certainties provided by hierarchy and an entire culture predicated on not complaining, I excelled. Cooking, for me, was the perfect balance of the mechanical with the human. You had to be like a robot, work like a robot, stay cool like a robot, all while utilizing your human senses: taste, touch, smell. That ability of soldiering through discomfort and pain, honed through childhood, began to pay off. I was the star pupil. During my first externship, a three-month stage at a small hotel called Auberge de la Valloire in a speck of a town in southeastern France called Épinouze, I worked through a nasty bout of mono. I was almost delirious with fatigue on the line but didn't miss a beat. My girlfriend at the time and I constituted the entire kitchen staff, and we didn't miss a plate. Not even mono could dampen the high I felt at having toughed it out.

When I returned to Chicago, I started to hear whispers about a local chef who had studied at Thomas Keller's The French Laundry, and was doing crazy things blocks away. I remember huddling around a computer in the college's computer room with a few other students looking at pictures on a forum called egullet of that chef, Grant Achatz, messing around at someone's (turned out future Alinea co-owner Nick Kokonas's) house. He hung a peeled grape, still on the vine, dipped it in peanut butter and wrapped it in a piece of toast. My mind was blown. It reminded me of dishes I had seen in the elBulli cookbook, which at $300 was the most expensive thing I owned. Later that year, when I was assigned a class project to design my own restaurant, I took inspiration from The French Laundry. Since I knew Grant had worked there, I arranged an interview with him so I could learn how a tasting menu worked. But when I arrived at the newly opened restaurant, he evidently hadn't gotten the email about the interview, and thought I was there looking for a stage. I didn't correct him. Soon enough, I was ushered back into the kitchen to make lavender balloons. At the end of that trial, Grant came up to me and asked, "When are you coming back?" I responded, "Whenever you want me to." I came back the next day, and I started to work at Alinea the day after that, two weeks after it opened.

For the next four years, that crucible of high pressure and even higher technique—not to mention culinary imagination—was my home, 14 hours a day, 5 days a week. I would have stayed forever, but even Alinea couldn't contain my ambition. Although I was always told we were the best restaurant in the world, I had to find out for myself. When I told Grant I was leaving, he understood. "Greg," he told me, "you're either going to realize you hated this place or that you loved it."

My next stop was a stage at Mugaritz, Andoni Luis Aduriz's avant-garde restaurant in San Sebastián, Spain. Although I didn't speak Spanish, again, I was the golden boy, with a digital translator next to my cutting board and a few key kitchen terms—*fuego*, *marcha*, *salmonete*—written out phonetically. After nearly five months, toward the end of the stage, my girlfriend, a pharmacist named Meghan I had met in Chicago, flew out to meet me. I proposed to her, she said yes. The future was bright for us. By this time, I had gotten a job offer at Thomas Keller's Per Se in New York. So we moved to New York, despite neither of us knowing anything about the big city.

Well, she moved to New York. I moved to a New York kitchen, which is different. I barely saw the city outside of it. Although Keller and his chefs

NORWICH MEADOWS FARM
NORW H MEADOWS FAR

de cuisine, first Jonathan Benno and then Eli Kaimeh, maintained blisteringly high standards (a sign reading "Sense of Urgency" still hangs on the kitchen threshold), again I thrived; again my penchant for hard work and gutting it out helped me excel. After a year and a half, and with assistance from Grant, another chef, Dan Barber, called me up and invited me to work at Blue Hill at Stone Barns, a two-star Michelin restaurant on a former Rockefeller family estate two hours north of the city.

At Blue Hill, the pattern repeated and, as far as I was concerned, there was no problem. Millions of hours, few days off. Head down. Hands in motion. Do it right or not at all. From Dan, a largely self-taught chef, I learned a reverence for simple ingredients. Early on, as Dan and I were walking in the fields surrounding the restaurant, he stopped suddenly and pulled a beautiful Hakurei turnip out of the ground. He held it up to me and said, triumphantly, "You can't get that at Per Se!" I laughed—his enthusiasm for ingredients was infectious.

I quickly worked my way to the top of the kitchen hierarchy at Blue Hill, and in 2013, feeling like I had learned all I could, I decided to leave. When an opportunity arose to work with the legendary restaurateur Danny Meyer and his chef, Floyd Cardoz, at North End Grill in downtown Manhattan, I took the job. Meanwhile, my personal life, such as it was, remained an afterthought. Meghan and I got divorced. She moved back to Chicago, and yet that hardly registered. As far as I was concerned, my life was going exactly to plan.

In 2016, at the age of thirty-one, I finally fulfilled my lifelong dream: I opened Olmsted, my own fine-dining restaurant, in Brooklyn, and probably the reason you're reading this book. Olmsted was the culmination of everything I had learned in the best kitchens in America, suffused with my own personal Midwest expression. We opened in the summer of 2016, with a garden humming with life, crawfish, quail, and critical buzz. Almost immediately, accolades poured in: *Esquire*'s Best New Restaurant, *GQ*'s Restaurant of the Year, and raves from Eater and the *New York Times*. I made it, I thought.

The volta. A volta is the part in a sonnet where everything changes. Vibes shift. The fate of our hero sours. Storm clouds on the horizon burst. Shit happens. When Olmsted opened, I thought my life would be clear. I had, after all, been working for my own restaurant for decades. And yet, nothing became clearer. If anything, I felt more lost, adrift, unmoored. One night, three years after we opened, I was so drunk in the kitchen office that I passed out and had to be snuck out the side so as not to alarm the guests. That I drank until I lost consciousness at the restaurant was a new low point, but that I was blackout drunk wasn't. I don't know when I had become an alcoholic, but I certainly had become one. A few months earlier, when my second restaurant, Maison Yaki, opened, I couldn't even hide from myself that I was unhappy. More than unhappy. I felt paralyzed. Beers, beers everywhere all the time, helped numb the sadness. I drank in the back of bodegas. In the bathrooms of my restaurants. At home. Everywhere. I knew I was spiraling and, in a moment of clarity, I thought, like a good Scout, "Okay, I'll do the right thing here." I found a therapist who diagnosed me as having massive depression and chronic anxiety. I was overjoyed. When I was prescribed SSRIs, a type of drug that helps lift the floor of depressive episodes, I thought all my problems were solved. But when the drugs seemed only to exacerbate my lows and did nothing to temper my highs, I returned to self-medicating, drinking more and more and more.

Shortly after the incident where I passed out at the restaurant, I decided to get sober. Without telling anyone at work—the shame monster!—I checked into an inpatient rehab in Palm Springs, California. Rehab was a lot. With all distractions removed—no phone, no Instagram, no emails—I was forced to look at myself. That, more than the absence of alcohol, was the most devastating. I didn't like what I saw. I had spent my life trying to be a chef who people looked up to, like Grant or Keller. But who could look up to who I had become? Eighteen years of nothing but cooking, no social life, few friends, no hobbies, had estranged me from the world. *Well*, I thought, *I can fix this*. Eager as always, I attended every meeting: AA, NA, Recovery Dharma, even Wellbriety, a form of addiction treatment for Indigenous people. I returned to New York sober for the first time in years. The only drugs I took were ones that were prescribed; the only drinks I would consume were vast quantities of coffee. This was the new Greg. I gathered my employees for a meeting at Olmsted, explained where I'd been, apologized for my behavior in the past, and promised to do better.

Then the pandemic hit. We shut down Olmsted and Maison Yaki in March 2020. We repurposed Olmsted into a trading post, selling groceries to keep the doors open and at least a few staff employed, and transformed Maison Yaki into a showcase for BIPOC creators. But I totally fell apart. Like many business owners and human beings, I found the pandemic enormously stressful. On top of that, I was still frustratingly alternating between lows so profound I couldn't get out of bed and flurries of manic activity. This was supposed to be fixed, I thought. So I did what I always did. I drank. And, because we were shut down, there was hardly anything stopping me from drinking myself to death.

As any alcoholic can tell you (at least the ones who live), at some point, a survival instinct kicks in. Now, whether you are too trashed or too far gone to heed it is another matter. But one night, I bought a one-way ticket to Chicago. If I stayed in New York I'd end up dead, by drink or my own hand.

When I got home, it got even worse. I didn't have the restaurants to run to and I wasn't used to lying to cover my drinking. There are plenty of sordid details of my own humiliation and bad behavior. The time I pissed myself in my bed. Or how during Oktoberfest I got a DUI in Illinois, where I begged the officers in jail not to call my dad, anyone but my dad, because I was too ashamed, because his own brother—after whom I was named—died by a drunk driver. When they did call him, and he picked me up, I bolted from his moving car and hid in the bushes before escaping to a Buffalo Wild Wings to drink more beer, before my sister, Katie, by this time an emergency room doctor, showed up in a fräulein outfit with four police officers in tow.

Any details from this evening I am piecing together from the few things I recall from that day and what others have told me. I had given up. I didn't care anymore. Somehow I convinced the cops to take me to a hotel. My plan was to call an Uber, head to O'Hare, and fly back to Brooklyn. As soon as they dropped me off, I found another bar and shoved down shitty wings and a couple more beers. That was probably the worst sleep I've ever had. Even after drinking a bottle of Nyquil hoping it would make me pass out, I didn't. Instead, I rolled around, tossing and turning, loathing everything about myself. I pictured not waking up. I pictured flinging myself from the bridge near my hotel. Everyone would be better off without me.

Again, my sister rescued me. Showing up unannounced, she sat me down and said, "Greg, I'm really worried about you. I'd like to admit you to a hospital and get a psych evaluation. I don't think this is just alcoholism and depression." That was the first time in over a year of actively seeking help that

ATHLETIC BREWING CO
La Croix
PAMPLEMOUSSE
LIME
HARBISON
CARA CARA MARMALADE
SEE A FARM
THE ORIGINAL
OAT-LY!
OAT-MILK
No dairy. No nuts. No gluten.
64 fl oz (1/2 GAL) (1.89L)
PEAR CHUTNEY
Ricotta
KETCHUP
FRESNO HOT SAUCE
EPIC DUCK FAT
Corn
Fennel
Eggplant
Brussels
Shiitake
Broccoli
Carrots

I felt hopeful. Maybe I wasn't just a drunk asshole, broken and forever useless.

The next morning, my sister and I headed for Northwestern Hospital in downtown Chicago. Katie did all the talking for me. She was more forthcoming than I would have been on my own. Listening to her, I learned how others had been seeing me. I had become a person I didn't recognize.

After talking to what felt like dozens of social workers, nurses, and doctors, I was given lunch: room-temperature pot roast, mashed potatoes, and carrots. As I ate my meal, I noticed that there was nothing in the room that someone could use to harm themselves, and I became aware that I was in a place for very seriously ill patients. The resident attending walked in and once again I explained why I was there. "Have you ever experienced rapid mood swings or have very high highs and low lows?" he asked. "Or put differently, do you ever find yourself to be excited, maybe even creative for a burst of time, then become tired, anxious, or irritated? Do you ever feel filled with anger one minute and fine the next?" "Um, yeah. That's me," I said. "Do you know what being bipolar means?" the doctor asked. *Oh shit!* I think to myself. "I believe I do," I responded. "We believe that you are bipolar and probably have been your entire life based on the information you provided. We'd like to adjust all your medications and begin treating you for mood disorder," says the doctor.

After the hospital I spent another four weeks in a rehab facility called The Ranch. No phones or electronics were allowed, but of course I snuck in a phone and made a couple calls to convey some messages and get any updates on the restaurants. A couple days later, I snuck a look at the phone again and got some anxiety-inducing news: I was also told that I had made a drunken call to someone in the food media while I was still in New York. It dawns on me that I remember setting up the call, but I don't remember the call itself. I was told I had also been shit-talking a high-profile chef. Needless to say, I went into a major panic. I wanted out of the treatment center ASAP. I wanted to die. I couldn't handle the shame. Despite many sessions of therapy, yoga nidra, hikes, and endless trays of nachos, I couldn't escape my sober thoughts: *Who the hell have you become?*

How many times do you really look in the mirror and make an honest appraisal of yourself? I'd bet not that often. I had managed to avoid that for my entire adult life, but during that stretch in rehab, there was no escape, and I didn't like what I saw. A combination of misdiagnosed bipolar disorder and alcoholism meant that at times I was the Eagle Scout, others profoundly not. When I was in the depths of depression, I was quick to anger, quick to reprimand, quick to think poorly of those around me. When I was drunk, or getting there, I hid, removing myself from my responsibilities and making others pick up my slack. All this, paired with the fact that I had spent most of my life in the high-pressure kitchens of the country's best restaurants where any weakness or failure is dealt with severely, turned me into an unpredictable volcano. I was coming to terms with the fact that those closest to me, and those forced to work with me, had borne the brunt of this.

I was a broken lonely man, a Jekyll and Hyde, an Eagle Scout and a drunk, a loser. And swirling around me, like vapors, I saw all the stories I told myself about myself, all that I had done to keep myself from seeing—from being with or in—myself. And I realized, nothing mattered. No stories I told myself about myself mattered. No pursuit possibly mattered, or could indemnify my behavior. The only thing that could set me free, that could dispel the fog of self-deception, was honesty, and that is what this book is about.

Nothing matters can be a real bummer of a thought. But over the last few years, I've come to use the mantra more like an air balloon, to remove some of the weight I've always felt on my shoulders. I am not the world's greatest chef and it doesn't matter. That entire dream—the delusion, really—that having a successful restaurant would make me happier doesn't matter. I'm not perfect. That's okay! Who is? Sometimes I'm sad. Sometimes I get lonely. Why cover it up? Who does that help? We all make mistakes, errors, have off-days, tantrums, burn things, undercook others, break vows and sauces, misread social cues and recipe amounts. What matters isn't that you fucked up but that, as so many cliché motivational posters have it, you get back up.

What matters is honesty, painful as it might be. So this is a radically honest cookbook. As my dad has always said, "Do a job big or small; do it right or not at all." Understanding my journey to sobriety and my struggles with mental health is important only because those struggles and that journey have catalyzed an honesty in me, an acceptance and a compassion that was hard-won. As you'll see in these pages, I'm still not perfect. And I'm honestly annoyed and exhausted and tired of reading all these aspirational lifestyle books wherein the author seems to be living their best life while the rest of us are out here struggling. I always thought, still think, that far from uplifting the reader, that can be alienating. So, this book is not that. It's Baxtrom, warts, loneliness, and all.

Over the years, I've been able to repair many of the relationships I ruined. But I can't go back in time, I can't undo what has been done. One thing that helps me come to terms with my past behavior is now doing what I can to be of service to others, a return to the values I learned as a Scout. So I think to myself, what can I offer? What lotuses can I call forth from the muck of having fucked up for so long? The answer is cooking. I can cook. That I know. The one thing that has literally kept me alive has been cooking. The joy I get from transforming raw ingredients into comforting, sustaining meals has not dimmed. Knowing nothing matters has freed me to rediscover that joy of cooking. I feel freer, lighter, more able to forgive myself in the kitchen and out of it. And that's what I want to share here.

In this book, I'm using all those years I've spent cooking to take out what actually matters and share it with you. I don't just mean technique, but really an honest evaluation of what is important in cooking and what isn't. Much of the fancy technique you see at restaurants doesn't *really* matter. You can get nearly the same effect with infinitely less work, and it's more fun and you might actually do it. Many of the tropes of fine-dining cookbook recipes—the hyperspecificity, the rigidity of the recipes—they don't matter, either.

This book is that: true. It's a little light and a little dark, very useful, sad sometimes, happy other times. And above all it's honest: about me, about my life, my experiences, the knowledge I've gained. I've tried to let my ego go here, to be honest and vulnerable, to share the food that I actually make the way I actually make it. And it will be delicious. You have my word, and, to me, that matters.

On my honor.

Greg Baxtrom

ecco
IDG
BOOKS
5098-5

STAPLES

Spices

FALL-A-KAKE
PX SPICE
PASILLA CHILI DRY RUB
BAXTROM SPICE
CITRUS SALT

Baxtrom Spice and Its Endless Uses

Makes 3½ cups • Prep time: 5 minutes • Cook time: n/a

1 cup kosher salt
½ cup freshly ground black pepper
½ cup paprika
½ cup dried oregano
½ cup onion powder
½ cup garlic powder

Back when I was a young fresh culinary school graduate, full of confidence and vim, I invited all my hometown friends over for dinner, eager to show off my newly minted cooking skills. I worked all afternoon, emerging from the kitchen with a platter of perfect golden chicken legs, speckled with a spice mix I had made using what I had at that time in the cabinet. They oohed. They aah'd. They cut open the chicken only to find it was . . . raw on the inside. Being both friends and polite Midwesterners, they gamely ate around the edges of the chicken, leaving me, when they left, with chunks of raw meat and a crisis of confidence. Well, at least the spice mix saved me, and it has continued to save me throughout my career. When I was in charge of family meal at Alinea, we reserved a space for a canister of Baxtrom Spice on the hallowed spice wall. Versatile, easy to source, and neutral enough to go with most things, this mix has never let me down.

In a bowl, whisk together the salt, pepper, paprika, oregano, onion powder, and garlic powder. Store in an airtight container for up to 6 months.

Uses

- Great on grilled chicken
- Perfect on pork roast
- Season the water you cook your rice in
- Put it in beans
- Fish!
- Veggies!

PX Spice

Makes 2 cups • Prep time: 1 minute • Cook time: n/a

1 cup freshly ground black peppercorns
½ cup freshly ground fennel seeds
½ cup freshly ground coriander

In restaurant lingo, to PX someone is to treat them like a VIP: send out a free midcourse treat or take extra care with a dish. Critics get PX'd. Celebrities get PX'd. Really good regulars get PX'd. It just means to add a little special touch. This spice mix PX's everything it touches. I use it as a substitute for black pepper when I'm looking to add a warming, comforting flavor. Try it: Open any cookbook, this one or another, pick a recipe, and sub in PX Spice for the black pepper. It instantly feels a little bit more special.

In a bowl, whisk together the peppercorns, fennel seeds, and coriander. Store in an airtight container for up to 6 months.

Note: Use a coffee or spice grinder to quickly grind the peppercorns and fennel seeds.

Uses

- Add to chili and corn bread
- Mix into a sausage blend
- Season a roast meat
- Swirl into salad dressing
- Dust atop sautéed broccoli rabe or glazed carrots

A NOTE ON INGREDIENTS:
UNLESS OTHERWISE SPECIFIED,
ALL MILK IS WHOLE
ALL BUTTER IS UNSALTED
ALL EGGS ARE MEDIUM
AND
ALL SALT IS DIAMOND CRYSTAL KOSHER SALT

Pasilla Chile Dry Rub

Makes about 1 cup • Prep time: 1 minute • Cook time: n/a

- ½ cup pasilla chile powder
- 1 tablespoon freshly ground black pepper
- 1 tablespoon ground fennel
- 1 tablespoon ground cumin
- 1 tablespoon ground coriander
- 1 tablespoon dried oregano
- 1 tablespoon dried thyme
- 1 teaspoon garlic powder
- 1 teaspoon smoked paprika

Think of this as slightly fancy taco seasoning. It has all the usual ingredients, but my version replaces the chili powder with ground pasilla chiles, and adds fennel. Pasilla is the name for the dried form of a chilaca chile, a long, narrow mild- to hot-flavored chile. (Beware: Anchos, the dried form of a poblano chile, are often mislabeled as pasilla, but they are wider and more stout.) Look for a pasilla powder that is vibrantly colored, which is a good indicator of freshness. It's the right amount of smoky without being bitter, the right amount of heat without being overpowering. Starting with ground spices is fine for this recipe, but if you want to pump up the flavors even more, try drying and grinding your own spices.

In a bowl, whisk together all the ingredients. Store in an airtight container for up to 3 months.

Uses

- Taco or fajita seasoning
- Sprinkle a little bit on scallops and roll them around on the grill (see Summer Scallop Succotash, page 174)
- Use as a spice base for chili
- Add to your House Pickling Liquid (page 38)
- Mix into the Homemade Mayonnaise (page 26) and let sit for a couple of hours
- Sprinkle over popcorn (see pages 77 to 79)

Fall-a-kake

Makes 4 cups • Prep time: 15 minutes • Cook time: 25 minutes

- Neutral oil, for deep-frying
- 1 bunch sage, leaves picked
- 1 cup wild rice
- 1 cup pumpkin seeds
- Extra-virgin olive oil
- Kosher salt and freshly ground black pepper
- One 1-ounce package nori
- Pinch of grated nutmeg

Traditional furikake is a Japanese dried seasoning with sesame seeds, nori, salt, and sugar. Here I've made a more autumnal furikake mixture with nori, salt, sage, pumpkin seeds, and nutmeg. Think of it is as Everything Spice, able to be used out of context for the betterment of all it touches.

Line a plate with paper towels and have near the stove. Pour four inches neutral oil into a medium saucepan and heat over medium until it reaches its smoke point (375° to 400°F).

Working in batches, carefully fry the sage leaves until crisp, about 10 seconds per leaf. Remove and set on the prepared plate to drain.

Line a large tray with paper towels and have near the stove. Let the oil return to its smoke point. Place ¼ cup of the wild rice in a fine-mesh sieve and lower the sieve into the hot oil until the grains puff up, a minute or so. Spread the rice on the prepared tray. Continue frying the remaining ¾ cup wild rice in ¼-cup batches.

Preheat the oven to 350°F.

In a bowl, toss the pumpkin seeds lightly in olive oil, salt, and pepper. Spread them out on a sheet pan and transfer to the oven. Bake until puffed, 15 to 20 minutes, shaking them halfway through.

To assemble the furikake, crumble together the nori and fried sage with your hands until the pieces are about the same size as the rice and pumpkin seeds. Add the nutmeg and stir to combine. (You can also just pulse everything in a food processor.)

Store the furikake in a zip-seal plastic bag or a glass jar. It'll keep for about 2 weeks in a cool, dry place.

Uses

- Think of fall-a-kake like furikake—that is, sprinkle it on top of rice
- Fold it into an aioli for a crunchy mayonnaise
- Add it on top of a salad, of course

Citrus Salt

Makes 1 cup • Prep time: 5 minutes • Cook time: n/a

1 cup salt: Maldon, Murray River, or Diamond Crystal kosher salt
Grated zest of 1 lemon
Grated zest of 1 lime
Grated zest of 1 orange
Grated zest of 1 grapefruit (optional)

Infused salts are instant culinary force multipliers, and this is one of my favorite all-purpose blends. The bright citrus flavor it imparts is delightful, it lasts up to a month, and it's easy to make. What's not to love? Depending on how I'm planning on utilizing the salt, I use either Murray River, Maldon, or regular kosher salt. If I'm using this mixture as a finishing salt, I prefer the lighter Murray River or large-flaked Maldon. But that can get expensive, so if I'm going to use this salt for curing, I'll use regular, cheaper, and higher-sodium kosher salt.

In a small bowl, whisk together the salt, lemon zest, lime zest, orange zest, and grapefruit zest (if using). Transfer to a 1-pint container. Citrus salt will keep for up to 1 month in the refrigerator.

Uses

- **Quick-Cured Tuna or Salmon with Citrus:** Make the citrus salt from scratch and hold on to the citrus fruits you zested. Use kosher salt in the mix, and season each side of a piece of tuna or salmon with the citrus salt and let it sit for 30 minutes. Rinse the fish under cold water until all the salt is removed and slice it to your desired thickness. Cut half the citrus you zested into segments and serve alongside the fish. Juice the other half of the citrus, mix the juice with an equal part of olive oil, and drizzle over the top of the fish along with whatever herbs you have lying around.
- **Citrus-Cured Salmon:** Clean a side of salmon, cover with the citrus salt, wrap in plastic, place on a sheet pan, and refrigerate. Flip it over at some point. Leave it for up to 12 hours. Then treat it like lox or a cured tartare.
- Use it as a finishing salt for a salad, like a beautiful mâche salad with goat cheese and roasted beets. That's a good idea.

Condiments

Floyd Cardoz's Pear Chutney

Makes 4 cups • Prep time: 15 minutes • Cook time: 45 minutes

- 2½ pounds Bartlett pears (6 medium), peeled, cored, and diced
- 2 cups apple cider
- ½ cup apple cider vinegar
- ½ cup golden raisins
- 3 medium shallots, diced
- 4 teaspoons grated peeled fresh ginger (grated on a Microplane)
- ½ head garlic (about 6 cloves), grated on a Microplane
- 1 serrano chile, minced
- ½ cup glucose syrup (see Note)
- 1 teaspoon ground turmeric
- 1 teaspoon brown mustard seeds
- 1 teaspoon yellow mustard seeds
- ½ teaspoon freshly ground black pepper
- 1 whole star anise, ground
- ⅛ teaspoon ground cardamom
- 1 teaspoon kosher salt, plus more as needed

Note: Glucose syrup can be sourced, like everything else, from Amazon. But if you don't want to support an evil monopoly, you can get it at a baking store. And if you don't want to do that, you can just swap in light corn syrup, though the chutney will be noticeably sweeter.

Chefs cook recipes from other chefs all the time. But for obvious reasons, they rarely talk about it. This chutney is different. This is Floyd Cardoz's chutney. I had the opportunity to cook with Floyd (who passed away from COVID in 2020) when he opened North End Grill in Battery Park City, in Manhattan, in 2012. I had just left Stone Barns and, while working as a ringer of a line cook through the critic review process—a common practice—Floyd was gracious enough to let me see how he and Danny Meyer opened a restaurant. (The restaurant got a glowing two-star review in the *New York Times*.) This began a friendship and late-career mentorship that lasted until his death. Floyd was a master of chutneys, an Indian condiment made from chopped fruit, vinegar, and spices, and his recipes always preserved the underlying flavor of the fruit while letting the delightful mix of spices shine.

This recipe counters the myth that everything is better cooked low and slow. The heat on this is medium-high. You have to go fast to keep the integrity of the fruit. You want it to taste like what it is. When I opened Olmsted, we made this chutney to accompany a duck salad with a red lentil naan. When we dropped the plate, we always said, "This is Chef Floyd's chutney."

In a large wide pot, combine the pears, cider, vinegar, raisins, shallots, ginger, garlic, chile, glucose syrup, turmeric, both mustard seeds, the black pepper, star anise, cardamon, and salt. Bring to a boil over high heat. Once boiling, reduce the heat to medium and allow it to simmer, stirring occasionally, until reduced by half, 40 to 45 minutes. Season with more salt to taste.

Let cool completely, then store in a sealed jar in the refrigerator for up to 1 month.

Uses

- Use for anything that calls for a condiment caught between sweet and savory
- Use on top of ice cream or French toast or atop a piece of baked fish or baked duck
- Puree the chutney and use as a foundation for a salad dressing

French's-ish Yellow Mustard

Makes 4 cups • Prep time: 10 minutes • Cook time: 10 minutes

1 cup yellow mustard seeds (see Note)
½ cup red wine vinegar
1 tablespoon kosher salt
1 tablespoon sugar
1½ teaspoons ground turmeric

Note: If you're interested in making Pickled Mustard Seeds (recipe follows)at the same time, double the amount of mustard seeds here and save half of them for the pickled mustard seeds recipe.

Of all the condiments to make at home, mustard is an easy win because it's incredibly simple to prepare. Also, it lasts a long time, and I like things that last a long time. As for why French's? In this bright yellow mustard, the astringency of the mustard seeds is removed by the cooking process. Adults like it. Kids like it. Everyone likes it. This version is a hybrid between French's and a Dijon, making it less sweet but more versatile. It works as well on a charcuterie board as in a mac and cheese, on a hamburger, or in a salad dressing.

In a pot, combine the mustard seeds with cold water to cover. Bring to a boil and then drain. Repeat four more times, using fresh cold water each time. Drain.

Place the blanched and drained mustard seeds into a blender and add ½ cup water, the vinegar, salt, sugar, and turmeric. Blend on high until smooth.

Let cool completely, then taste and adjust the seasoning (add more vinegar, salt, or sugar as needed). Store the mustard in an airtight container in the refrigerator. It can last months.

PICKLED MUSTARD SEEDS

Makes 1 cup • Prep time: 15 minutes • Cook time: 30 minutes

Pickled mustard seeds, like mustards, last a long time and can be used to accompany a charcuterie board, to add balance to a stroganoff, or whenever you need a little burst of flavor: in a mayo with the mustard itself, as mustard caviar, in a dressing for a sandwich . . . the possibilities are endless.

1 cup yellow mustard seeds
2 cups House Pickling Liquid (page 38)

In a pot, combine the mustard seeds with cold water to cover. Bring to a boil and then drain. Repeat four more times, using fresh cold water each time. Drain.

In the same pot, bring the house pickling liquid to a boil over medium heat.

Place the drained blanched mustard seeds into a heatproof bowl. Pour the boiling pickling liquid on top. Let sit, covered, for a day at room temperature before using. Store in an airtight container in the refrigerator for up to 3 months.

Heirloom Pepper Hot Sauce

Makes about 3 cups • Prep time: 10 minutes • Cook time: n/a • Inactive time: 1 week

- 24 Fresno peppers (1 pound 2 ounces)
- 5 assorted other chiles, such as Thai chiles, jalapeño, or ají dulce peppers (2 to 3 ounces)
- 3 garlic cloves, peeled but whole
- 1 tablespoon kosher salt
- 2 cups distilled white vinegar

I grew up in a house where black pepper was considered spicy, so it goes without saying that I didn't grow up eating hot sauce. It wasn't until I got to culinary school and started to eat so-called ethnic food that I realized I couldn't handle the heat. So, in typical Eagle Scout fashion, I started to train myself, starting with Tabasco sauce, then graduating to serranos and habaneros, and finally ending with Armageddon peppers, with a Scoville rating of 1.3 million SHU, 400 times hotter than a jalapeño. Through sheer dedication, I increased my tolerance so that I could enjoy spicy larb, mapo tofu, kimchi. But when I stopped drinking, my ability to withstand heat returned to Illinois-suburb levels. (Among the many things alcohol numbs, one is the palate.) And so I began again. But that's just me. If you want a more gradual introduction, this hot sauce is mellow and variable. The bulk of it is made with Fresno peppers, a beginner chile with a bright red hue, but the remainder can be—should be—spicier: Thai chiles, jalapeños, habaneros, serranos, whatever you can get at the farmers' market. The bite and the pleasing complexity of the sauce comes not only from the peppers but from the fermentation, which takes place over the course of a week's time.

Cut the Fresnos and assorted chiles in half, remove the stems, and place in a food processor. Add the garlic and blitz until finely chopped. Transfer to an airtight container and stir in the salt. Cover and leave at room temperature for 1 week, mixing once a day.

After a week, transfer the mixture to a blender with the vinegar and puree on high until smooth.

Strain through a fine-mesh sieve, pressing against the solids to extract as much liquid as possible. Store in an airtight container. This will last in the refrigerator for 3 weeks.

A GOOD RULE OF THUMB ABOUT FERMENTATION: WEIGH THE THING YOU WANT TO FERMENT, THEN USE 2% OF ITS WEIGHT IN SALT. THE SALT WILL PULL MOST OF THE WATER OUT OF WHATEVER YOU'RE FERMENTING, AND THAT SALTY WATER BECOMES THE BRINE. THE LONGER IT SITS, THE MORE SOUR IT'LL BE.

Homemade Mayonnaise

Makes about 3 cups • Cook time: 1 hour

- 4 large egg yolks
- 3 tablespoons white wine vinegar
- 2 tablespoons Roasted Garlic Puree (see page 27)
- 1 tablespoon Dijon mustard
- 2 teaspoons kosher salt
- 2 cups (400 g) neutral oil

This is an old Alinea recipe that's super versatile and easy to remember: 4 eggs to 400 grams of oil, which works out to 2 cups. The mayonnaise itself is relatively neutral, so you can use it in many ways: as a sandwich spread, as a binder in a pasta or chicken salad, or slathered on a piece of chicken before you grill it or onto the outside of a grilled cheese before it goes into a pan. It also takes on other flavors really well, like Thai spices, yuzu koshō, Calabrian chile, or pickled mustard seeds (see Variations, page 27). Exactly how much water you use is up to you. This recipe as written gives you a standard mayo consistency, but if you're making the mayonnaise for coleslaw, omit the water entirely since the cabbage lets out a lot of liquid.

By hand: In a bowl, combine the egg yolks, vinegar, garlic puree, mustard, salt, and 2 tablespoons water and whisk together until incorporated. Slowly drizzle in the oil, whisking constantly, until the mixture is thick and emulsified.

With a food processor: In a food processor, combine the egg yolks, vinegar, garlic puree, mustard, salt, and 2 tablespoons water and blitz until combined. With the machine running, slowly drizzle in the oil until the mixture is thick and emulsified.

With an immersion blender: Place egg yolks, vinegar, garlic puree, mustard, salt, 2 tablespoons water, and oil in a tall glass and use an immersion blender to blend together. As you blend, slowly pull out the stick to emulsify the mayo.

THAI MAYONNAISE

Makes about 3 cups • Prep time: 5 minutes • Cook time: n/a

- 4 egg yolks
- 5 tablespoons Thai Dressing (page 111)
- ½ teaspoon kosher salt
- 1 cup fresh basil, roughly chopped
- 2 cups neutral oil

By hand: Place the egg yolks, Thai Dressing, salt, basil, and 2 tablespoons water into a bowl, then whisk together until incorporated. Slowly drizzle in the oil, whisking constantly, until the mixture is thick and emulsified.

With a food processor: Place the egg yolks, Thai Dressing, salt, basil, and 2 tablespoons water into a food processor and blitz until combined. With the machine running, slowly drizzle in the oil until the mixture is thick and emulsified.

With an immersion blender: Place the egg yolks, Thai Dressing, salt, basil, 2 tablespoons water, and the oil into a tall glass and use an immersion blender to blend together. As you blend, slowly pull out the stick to emulsify the mayo.

FOR THE ROASTED GARLIC PUREE, ALL YOU HAVE TO DO IS CUT THE TOP AND TIP OFF THE HEAD OF GARLIC WRAP TIGHTLY IN FOIL & PLACE IN OVEN AT 350F FOR ABOUT AN HOUR. ONCE IT'S COOLED SQUISH IT THROUGH SOMETHING LIKE A COLANDER. THIS ALSO SEPARATES THE SKINS. DISCARD THE SKINS AND PUT THE GARLIC IN A BOWL WITH A LITTLE BIT OF SALT, PEPPER AND OLIVE OIL.

Variations

- **Yuzu Mayo:** Blend in 2 teaspoons yuzu koshō.
- **Spicy Mayo:** Blend in 3 tablespoons Calabrian chile paste.
- **Mustardy Mayo:** Blend in 2 tablespoons mustard and 3 tablespoons Pickled Mustard Seeds (page 24).

Tomato Red Onion Ketchup

Makes 1½ cups • Prep time: 5 minutes • Cook time: 25 minutes

- 5 Roma tomatoes, roughly chopped
- 1 medium red onion, roughly chopped
- 3 garlic cloves, peeled but whole
- ¼ cup distilled white vinegar, plus more as needed
- ¼ cup sugar, plus more as needed
- ¼ cup light corn syrup
- ⅛ teaspoon ground allspice
- ⅛ teaspoon ground cloves
- 1 teaspoon kosher salt, plus more as needed

Most ketchup is tomato-based, but it doesn't have to be. What makes ketchup *ketchup* is the balance between the base, sugar, and vinegar. This base recipe works with anything tomato-y—green tomatoes, red tomatoes, tomatillos—but it's equally delicious with cherries, strawberries, and even fermented cabbage. (If you're adding something else, just swap out half the tomatoes.) Each yields a unique flavor. The trick to a bright ketchup is that you want to boil it hard so the moisture is removed quickly and you get a full-bodied flavor. It's scary to go hard like this, and at times the mixture will look like unappetizing molten lava, but it's also the secret to a good ketchup. And once you've made it, thanks to the vinegar and the sugar, ketchup can last almost indefinitely.

In a food processor, combine the tomatoes, onion, and garlic and pulse together, scraping down the sides of the bowl a few times, until everything is finely chopped.

In a medium pot, combine the tomato/onion/garlic paste, vinegar, sugar, corn syrup, allspice, cloves, and salt and bring to a boil over medium-high heat. Reduce the heat to low and simmer until reduced by half, 20 to 22 minutes.

Let cool slightly, then return to the food processor and blend again. Drain in a chinois or a fine-mesh sieve. Set aside to cool completely.

Once it's cooled, season with additional salt, vinegar, or sugar to taste. Ketchup can last months in an airtight container in the refrigerator.

Variations

- **Cherry Ketchup:** Sub out half the tomatoes for the same amount of pitted fresh cherries.
- **Strawberry Ketchup:** Sub out half the tomatoes for same amount of hulled strawberries.
- **Sauerkraut Ketchup:** Sub out half the tomatoes for the same amount of Red Cabbage Sauerkraut (page 33).

Blood Orange Sweet and Sour Sauce

Makes 1½ cups • Prep time: 5 minutes • Cook time: 30 minutes

- 1 cup blood orange juice or regular orange juice
- 1 cup light corn syrup
- ½ cup sugar
- ½ cup rice vinegar
- 1 Fresno chile, halved lengthwise
- 3 garlic cloves, smashed (no need to peel)
- 2 green onions, thinly sliced
- 1 (2-inch) thumb fresh ginger, peeled and thinly sliced
- 1 tablespoon coriander seeds
- 2 teaspoons kosher salt, plus more as needed

Half my life is trying to sound good on a menu. Half of any chef's life. Hence using blood orange for this recipe, which sounds fancier than orange orange. But basically, it doesn't matter what you use! Anything citrusy or fruity will work. At Olmsted, we had a complicated sweet-and-sour sauce made with twenty-eight ingredients that we serve with crab Rangoon. This tastes similar, but with like half the ingredients. Also, it doesn't go bad.

In a saucepot, combine the blood orange juice, corn syrup, sugar, vinegar, chile, garlic, green onions, ginger, coriander seeds, and salt and bring to a boil over medium-high heat. Once boiling, reduce to medium heat and simmer until thickened slightly and reduced by a little more than half, 20 to 25 minutes, skimming the yellow/brown pulp from the top along the way.

Strain and let cool to room temperature, then season with salt to taste. Store in an airtight container for a few weeks.

Uses

– As a dipping sauce

– On pork nuggets (see page 156), chicken nuggets . . . really any nuggets

– Especially good with anything fried, like tempura-fried anything (see page 45)

Preserved Lemons

Makes 2 quarts • Prep time: 5 minutes • Cook time: n/a • Inactive time: 1 month

6 lemons
2 cups kosher salt
2 cups sugar

Bracingly tart and salty, a little bit of lemon preserve goes a long way. The combination of sweetness from the sugar and sour from the salty lemons will brighten up any mayo, soup, sauce, or dressing.

Wash and dry the lemons. Cut them in half lengthwise.

In a medium bowl, mix together the salt and sugar.

Toss the lemons in the salt mixture and empty the whole bowl's contents into a 1-gallon zip-seal plastic bag, removing as much air as possible before you seal. (Doing it in a bag, as opposed to a jar, means you can more easily squish around the lemons.)

Refrigerate for 1 month before using. Roll them around at least once a week to evenly distribute the ingredients.

Lemon preserves last in the fridge forever—they're preserved. But let's just say, try to eat them within a few months. It won't be difficult: They're delicious.

Uses

- **Lemony Mayo:** Remove the lemon seeds from about one preserved lemon, dice, then fold ¼ cup of the diced lemons into 1 cup mayo.
- Make a lemon butter (great for fish!) by removing the pith from the preserved lemons, dicing the rind, and adding it, with a little bit of the lemony preserving liquid, to a beurre monté (see page 187)
- Dice the rind and add to rice before you cook it
- It goes great in yogurt for a healthy breakfast
- Or how about using the juice in which the lemons sit as a seasoning liquid? That's a good idea.

IF YOU DON'T WANT TO WAIT A WHOLE MONTH, PUT THE LEMONS IN THE FREEZER, THEN LET THEM THAW IN THE FRIDGE. REPEAT THIS PROCESS EVERYDAY FOR A WEEK. THE WATER MOLECULES, WHEN FROZEN, PIERCE THE FLESH OF THE LEMON, PENETRATING THEM DEEPLY. WITH EVERY REPETITION OF THE PROCESS, IT CUTS DEEPER. IT'S LIKE HAVING THE SAME FIGHT OVER AND OVER AGAIN BUT WITH A HAPPY ENDING!

Whole Citrus Marmalade

Makes 1 pint • Prep time: 10 minutes • Cook time: 1 hour 30 minutes

6 medium oranges (about 2 pounds; see below)
4 cups sugar

YOU CAN BASICALLY USE ANY CITRUS FOR THIS. THE IDEA IS TO KEEP THE RATIO OF SUGAR TO JUICE TO PULP 1:1:1 SO 4 CUPS SUGAR TO 4 CUPS JUICE TO 4 CUPS BLITZED CITRUS PULP.

We had a rule at Olmsted: We didn't use any juice more than two days old. We went through a lot of citrus and sometimes had a lot of leftover juice. For a long time, the leftover citrus rinds would just go to compost and the leftover bar juice would get tossed. But one day, our pastry chef, Alex Grunert, shared this recipe for a marmalade that uses the entire citrus rind plus all the juice we could. We started doing it with all the lemon and lime we had left over, and the resultant marmalade tasted like Sprite, a plus. In the winter, we'd do it with blood oranges (fancy!) or grapefruit (less fancy, still fun!).

Juice the fruit and strain out the seeds. Ideally, you'll get 3 cups juice. You need 4 cups liquid, so whatever you don't have in juice can be replaced with store-bought juice or water. Set aside.

Place the spent citrus rinds in a large pot, cover completely with water, and bring to a boil over high heat. Once boiling, drain and rinse under cold water. Repeat this process four more times to remove any bitterness from the rinds.

After the fifth and final time, place the drained rinds in a food processor and blitz until finely chopped (work in batches if necessary).

Measure out 4 cups of the blitzed pulp and add it to the same pot. Add the reserved juice and sugar and bring to a boil over medium-high heat. Once boiling, reduce the heat to medium and cook, stirring occasionally (more often toward the end), until the liquid is mostly evaporated and the mixture is jammy, 20 to 30 minutes.

Remove from the heat and let cool. Store the marmalade in jars in the refrigerator for up to 1 month.

Uses

- Fold it into an aioli or into a hollandaise to make a sauce Maltaise
- Use in a salad dressing
- Use it on a sundae or ricotta toast
- Add it to the Blood Orange Sweet and Sour Sauce (page 29) to make it chunkier

Red Cabbage Sauerkraut

Makes 2 quarts • Prep time: 10 minutes • Cook time: n/a • Inactive time: 1 to 2 weeks

1 pound red cabbage, shredded
1 tablespoon kosher salt

Most sauerkraut is cooked, but not all and not mine. As it turns out, cooking kills many of the probiotics. Just like hot sauce, this is a simple ferment: 2% salt by weight and 1 week to ferment. We did a similar sauerkraut at Blue Hill at Stone Barns, but here I use red cabbage instead of white. (Whoa! Original.) The sauerkraut lasts for a loooong time. I'm not saying you should do this, but mine's been in my fridge for years.

Place the cabbage in a large bowl and rub the salt into the cabbage extremely well, massaging it with your hands. Add ¼ cup water. Cover the bowl tightly with plastic wrap. Then weight down the cabbage with a heavy bowl of fruit or potatoes or something. (Look, you can also just put the cabbage in a zip-seal bag and press it down.)

Let the cabbage sit out at room temperature for 1 to 2 weeks, depending on how funky you want it. 1 week = Jamiroquai; 2 weeks = James Brown. Every other day, stir, then reseal and reweight it down.

Uses

- Goes great on pierogies (see page 193)
- Add to a charcuterie board
- Serve with spaetzle (see page 186) and anything vaguely Germanic

How to Brine Anything

Makes 4 quarts (good for up to 10 pounds of protein) • Prep time: 10 minutes • Cook time: 10 minutes

Everything Brine

- 2 cups kosher salt
- 2 tablespoons plus 1 teaspoon pink curing salt
- 1 cup sugar
- 2 bay leaves, dried or fresh
- 1 garlic clove, whole
- 2 tablespoons fennel seeds
- 2 tablespoons coriander seeds
- ¼ cup black peppercorns
- ½ bunch tarragon
- Peel of 1 orange

Brining sounds intimidating, but it's basically just marinating, and marinating is just putting something in a liquid for a while. How hard is that? You take baths, don't you? The idea of a brine is that it not only preserves the protein but imparts flavor. A brine, especially one as rich in aromatics as this one, replaces any gaminess or irony (that is, a ferric) flavor with wonderful flavor, which is why I use this with everything from corned beef tongue and beef heart to duck pastrami and short ribs. However, I would not use it on fish, since it is too assertively salty for so delicate a flavor.

In a large pot, combine 4 quarts water, the kosher salt, pink curing salt, sugar, bay leaves, garlic, fennel seeds, coriander seeds, peppercorns, tarragon, and orange peel. Bring to a boil over medium heat and boil for 5 minutes.

Remove from the heat and let cool. Once cool, pour the brine over whatever you want, making sure you have enough to submerge the protein fully. You can brine the protein in the fridge for between 48 hours and up to 1 week before cooking.

How to Pickle Some Things

Although it's incredibly easy to make pickles, there are still some fundamentals to know. One is choosing the right vinegar. You can never go wrong with distilled white vinegar, but sometimes, if you want it to be a little fancier for, say, pickled beets, then you can use another vinegar, such as red wine vinegar, to complement the other ingredients. When pickling green vegetables, such as cucumbers, I prefer white wine vinegar or champagne vinegar, but again, distilled white vinegar works, too.

Then spices come into play. You basically can't make a wrong decision here, unless you start pulling out the cinnamon. Otherwise, anything in your spice cabinet will make for an interesting pickle. For example, some old oregano you have lying around works great. That ground ginger you have from Thanksgiving could make for some really good pickled green beans. I personally use PX Spice (page 19) in many of my pickle recipes. I do this because of course I love the flavor, but it's also an easy way to give a common ingredient everyone knows—the thing you are pickling—a subtle twist.

HOUSE PICKLING LIQUID

Makes 2½ cups

1 cup vinegar: red wine, distilled white, or white wine
1 cup sugar
1 tablespoon kosher salt
1 tablespoon of whatever spices you have lying around

In a pot, combine the vinegar, 1 cup water, the sugar, salt, and spices and bring to a boil. Allow to slightly cool, around 5 minutes, then pour over the ingredients you want to pickle.

Some Things to Pickle

PICKLED RADISHES

Makes 1 pint

1 bunch radishes, halved, most of the greens removed (though I like to leave a bit of the stem on)

House Pickling Liquid (page 38) made with red wine vinegar

Bring a pot of salted water to a boil. Add the radishes and blanch for 2 minutes. Drain the radishes before combining with the cooled pickling liquid.

Pickled radishes can last 1 month in the fridge and up to 1 year if canned properly. The longer they sit, the better.

PICKLED RASPBERRIES

Use these in the No-Big-Deal Roasted Beet Salad (page 53) and the Pickled Raspberry Shrub (page 210).

Makes about 2 cups

1 pint raspberries, rinsed

House Pickling Liquid (page 38) made with red wine vinegar

Pickled raspberries can last a month in the fridge and up to 1 year if canned properly. The longer they sit, the better.

PICKLED SHALLOTS

Makes 1 pint

5 shallots, peeled and thinly sliced on a mandoline

House Pickling Liquid (page 38), made with red wine vinegar

Pickled shallots can last 1 month in the fridge and up to 1 year if canned properly. The longer they sit, the better.

PICKLED CHERRIES

Use these in the Roasted Chicken Crown (page 129).

Makes 2 cups

1 pint cherries, stemmed, pitted, and torn in half

House Pickling Liquid (page 38), made with red wine vinegar

Pickled cherries can last 1 month in the fridge and up to 1 year if canned properly. The longer they sit, the better.

PICKLED CELERY

Use in the Buffalo Chicken Schnitzel Sandwich (page 119).

Makes 1 pint

4 celery stalks, cut on a bias into ½-inch-thick *Star Trek* logos

House Pickling Liquid (page 38), made with distilled white vinegar

Pickled celery can last 1 month in the fridge and up to 1 year if canned properly. The longer it sits, the better.

Bread and Butter Pickles

Makes about 1 quart • Inactive time: 14 hours • Prep time: 10 minutes • Cook time: 5 minutes

- 2 cucumbers (about 1 pound)
- ½ cup kosher salt
- 2½ cups apple cider vinegar
- 2½ cups granulated sugar
- 1 Spanish onion, thinly sliced
- 2 teaspoons yellow mustard seeds
- 2 teaspoons fennel seeds
- 2 teaspoons celery seeds
- 2 teaspoons ground turmeric

Not everyone wants a sour pickle. Or even a half-sour. Sometimes life is so sour already all you want is a little bit of sweetness in your pickle. Half pickle; half candy. Or here, thanks to Morgan Schofield, the original butcher at Olmsted, whose recipe this is, three-fifths pickle and two-fifths candy. (The pickle isn't quite as sweet as the store-bought ones.) Sure, the bread and butter pickle—so-called because when they were developed in Appalachia in the 1920s, they were so popular they could be traded for household staples like bread and butter—is the most lowbrow pickle. But it's also the most versatile. They work great on a burger or on a sandwich or, really, with any meat. Because they're made with small cucumbers and cut into coins (as opposed to spears), they work on a charcuterie board or as a snack with curried nuts.

Place the cucumbers in a deep-sided dish, such as a baking pan. Bring 2 quarts water and the salt to a boil and stir to dissolve, then pour over the cucumbers. Let sit at room temperature overnight, weighing down the cucumbers, if needed, with a pan to keep them submerged. After 12 hours, lift the cucumbers from the liquid, then pour the liquid into a large pot. Add the apple cider vinegar, sugar, onion, mustard seeds, fennel seeds, celery seeds, and turmeric to the pickling liquid and bring to a boil, stirring until the sugar dissolves. Meanwhile, slice the cucumbers into ¼-inch-thick coins and transfer to heatproof jars. Once the liquid has come to a boil, pour over the cucumbers to cover completely. Let cool completely at room temperature, about 2 hours, then seal the jars. Store in the refrigerator for months, honestly.

Two Very Good Ways to Fry

My first taste of the professional kitchen was at the Wendy's on the corner of 191st Street and Route 45 in Frankfort, Illinois. A bunch of friends and I all applied at the same time when we turned fifteen. I worked the fry station and immediately began experimenting: wrapping a nugget in bacon, for instance, and putting it on a skewer. None of my creations made the menu, obviously, but the experience did imbue me with a profound love of the deep-fried.

I love all types of frying, which basically fall into two categories: battered *or* breaded. Breading and frying is best for meats that can withstand a sauce. We'll get to that in Purple-Top Turnip Parm-less Parm (page 100) and pork nuggets later (see page 156). But within batter-frying, I want to discuss two of my favorite techniques. What I like most about the batter-fried process is that once you get a recipe for a batter down, you can use it for anything. I think the Beer Batter (page 45), with a richness from the beer, works best on fish and vegetables. One of the lightest ways to fry something is with Tempura Batter (page 45), a Japanese technique originally brought by the Portuguese in the seventeenth century. Although tempura was originally used only for vegetables, these days you—well, I mean, I—tempura everything: chicken, scallops, haricots verts, cauliflower, random stuff I have in my fridge. The trick is to cut everything up into pinky-finger sizes before frying. I use an old Alinea recipe, which, before that, was an old French Laundry recipe. At Alinea we'd have a little squab breast I'd tempura with a brown sugar pâte de fruits with a roasted shallot, skewered on an oak leaf branch. Not only was it my job to fry the squab, but it was part of my mise en place to source the oak leaves. It being winter in Chicago, the only place to find intact foliage was often under parked cars, so you could find me on my hands and knees in the snow looking for future skewers on freezing afternoons. Was it worth it? Abso-fucking-lutely. If you don't happen to have oak leaves handy, that's okay.

BEER BATTER

Makes 6 cups • Prep time: 10 minutes

You can make the beer batter mix ahead of time. Feel free to make two or three times the recipe and then store in a zip-seal bag. When you want to fry something, measure out 3¼ cups and add the liquid.

Beer Batter Mix

2 cups all-purpose flour, plus more for tossing
1 cup cornstarch
1 tablespoon garlic powder
1 tablespoon onion powder
1 tablespoon cayenne pepper
1 tablespoon sugar
½ teaspoon kosher salt

Beer Batter

One 12-ounce can pilsner (1½ cups), chilled
One 12-ounce can sparkling water (1½ cups), chilled

Make the beer batter mix: In a large bowl, whisk together the flour, cornstarch, garlic powder, onion powder, cayenne, sugar, and salt.

Make the batter: In a separate bowl, whisk together the pilsner and sparkling water until smooth. Slowly whisk the liquid ingredients into the dry ones until well incorporated.

I KEEP A POT OF OIL I'VE USED WITH FRYING HANGING OUT ON THE STOVE. IF THERE'S SCHMUTZ IN THERE I'LL STRAIN IT. IF YOU STRAIN ALONG THE WAY, THE SAME OIL KEEPS FOR ABOUT FIVE FRIES.

TEMPURA BATTER

Makes 2 cups • Prep time: 1 minute

You can make the tempura mix ahead of time. Feel free to make two or three times the recipe and then store in a zip-seal bag for months. When you want to fry something, measure out 1 cup and add the liquid.

Tempura Batter Mix

2 tablespoons baking powder
1 cup all-purpose flour
3 tablespoons cornstarch
1 cup sparkling water

Make the tempura batter mix: In a bowl, whisk together the baking powder, flour, and cornstarch.

Make the batter: In a bowl, whisk together the tempura mix and sparkling water until well incorporated.

HOW TO BATTER-FRY ANYTHING

1. Fill up your Dutch oven or heavy-bottomed cast-iron pot with about four inches of neutral oil. Heat over medium heat until it reaches 350°F.
2. Season what you want to be fried with salt, then toss in flour. Shake off the excess and dip into the batter. You want a thin coat, so scrape off excess before adding to the oil.
3. Fry for 2 to 4 minutes a side, until light golden. The denser the fryee, the longer the frying.
4. Remove and sprinkle with salt while hot.

SALADS

Cherry Tomato Salad with Sunkist Orange Juice

Serves 4 • Prep time: 25 minutes • Cook time: 10 minutes

3 tablespoons raisins
½ cup trimmed and quartered red radishes (4 ounces)
1 pint cherry tomatoes, halved
½ English cucumber (7 ounces), diced
¼ cup Pickled Shallots (page 39)
1 tablespoon Preserved Lemons (page 31), pith removed and minced
1 clementine, peeled and segments separated
¼ cup oil-packed sun-dried tomatoes, lifted from the oil and diced
½ cup Sunkist orange juice
2 tablespoons red wine vinegar
3 tablespoons extra-virgin olive oil
Kosher salt and freshly ground black pepper
½ cup homemade Little Curd Ricotta (see page 72) or store-bought
2 tablespoons honey
½ bunch basil, leaves picked (½ cup loosely packed), chiffonaded

When I was working at Stone Barns, Dan Barber had a savory, bright, acidic, and refreshing salad on the summer menu that was a runaway hit. After I left the restaurant, I used to try to make the salad at home whenever I entertained, but I never quite got it right. Then I happened upon the secret ingredient: Instead of using fresh orange juice, I began using Sunkist orange juice. Nailed it. What makes this salad shine is the mixture of oil from the sun-dried tomatoes, tomato juices from the fresh tomatoes, vinegar, olive oil, and orange juice. This forms a *caisson*—a fancy word for broth—at the bottom of the bowl, like a secret gazpacho awaiting you.

In a small pot, combine the raisins with cold water to cover. Bring to a boil over high heat. Allow to cool in the water, then drain and set aside.

Fill the small pot again, this time with salted water, and bring to a boil over high heat. Add the radishes and blanch for 2 minutes. Drain and set aside to cool.

In a large bowl, combine the raisins, cooled radishes, tomatoes, cucumber, shallots, Preserved Lemons, clementine, and sun-dried tomatoes. Stir in the orange juice, red wine vinegar, and 1 tablespoon of the olive oil. Season to taste with salt and pepper. Toss to combine, then place in the refrigerator for 30 minutes.

Meanwhile, blend together the ricotta, honey, and the remaining 2 tablespoons of olive oil in the bowl of a food processor until smooth.

To serve, schmear 2 tablespoons ricotta along the side of half of each of four plates. Toss the tomato salad once more, then equally divide among the four plates. Top with the basil and serve.

No-Big-Deal Roasted Beet Salad with Pickled Raspberries

Serves 4 as a side • Prep time: 25 minutes • Cook time: 1 hour

2 bunches red beets, tops attached
1 garlic head, halved horizontally
Extra-virgin olive oil
Kosher salt and freshly ground black pepper
½ cup Greek whole yogurt (optional)
½ pint Pickled Raspberries (page 39)

Dan Barber had a roasted beet salad with pine nuts, mâche, and raspberry vinegar on the menu at Blue Hill, and the combination of sweet, tart, and earthy flavors always stuck with me. I thought back to that combination when I first made this salad after putzing around at the farmers' market. Zaid and Brant from Norwich Meadow Farms gave me a bag full of beets and raspberries to fool around with. I wanted to cook, but it was hot and I was lazy, so the no-big-deal salad was born.

Pickling raspberries is one of those processes that sounds fancy and, you know, isn't really (see page 39). As a bonus, the pickling liquid of the raspberries intermingles with the olive oil of the dressing to make a raspberry vinaigrette of sorts. Don't overthink it.

Oh, and because I had a lot of leftover raspberries, I made a Raspberry Shrub (page 210) to accompany the salad. You should, too.

Preheat the oven to 350°F.

Remove the tops of the beets and wash both beets and tops separately in cold water. Set the tops aside.

Remove the cloves of garlic from the head, saving 1 clove for your garlic fork (it'll make sense in a sec). Add the garlic to a bowl along with the beets, adding enough olive oil to coat everything. Season with salt and pepper. Wrap the beets tightly in one big foil packet.

Bake until done, about 1 hour. There are two ways to check whether a beet is done. One is to insert a knife. If done, there should be little resistance. The other is to remove the beets from the oven and, while they're warm, use a shitty towel to rub off the skin. If the skin comes off easily, your beet is done. If not, put them back in the oven.

Once the beets are done and cool enough to handle, peel and cut the beets into thumb-size chunks and set aside.

In a sauté pan, heat a splash of olive oil over medium heat until shimmering. Spear the reserved garlic clove with a fork. Add the reserved beet tops to the pan, stirring with the garlic fork. Season to taste with salt and pepper and remove once wilted. (They can be served warm or cool, doesn't matter.)

If using yogurt, season it well with salt and lots of black pepper. Then begin plating by swooshing some on a plate. Then alternate layers of beets and their greens atop the plate. Finish with the Pickled Raspberries, using two tablespoons of their liquid as a vinaigrette for the beet salad. Finish with a drizzle of olive oil.

How to "break" pickled raspberries: Store any leftover raspberries in a sealed container in the refrigerator for up to 1 month. A common restaurant trick is to "break" the pickled raspberries with olive oil, which means simply store the pickled raspberries with a layer of olive oil on top. That way, when you scoop into the jar to get them, you're functionally scooping back out a vinaigrette.

WHAT THE HELL IS A GARLIC FORK?

• A BRILLIANT WAY TO IMPART GARLIC FLAVOR TO WHATEVER YOU'RE STIRRING.

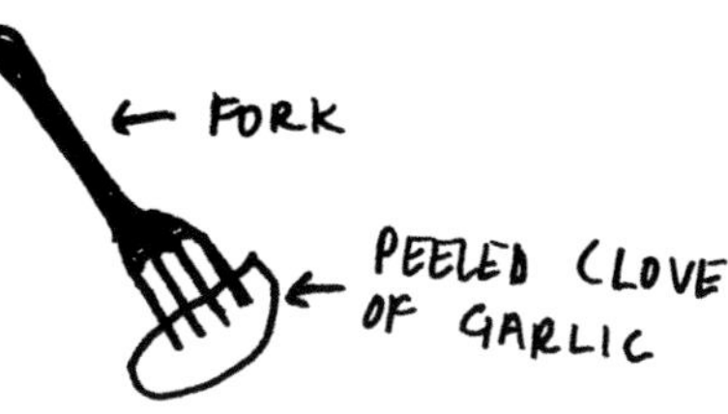

Lemony Kale Salad

Serves 4 • Prep time: 25 minutes • Cook time: 20 minutes

Croutons

2 cups bread cubes (leftover hamburger buns, sourdough, challah cut into ½-inch cubes)
¼ cup extra-virgin olive oil
Kosher salt and freshly ground black pepper
PX Spice (page 19)

Salad

2 red radishes, trimmed and thinly sliced
One (5-ounce) clamshell baby kale (sorry for the plastic!)
¼ cup Pickled Shallots (page 39)
Rucolish Dressing (recipe follows)
Freshly grated Parmesan cheese, for serving

Obviously, I don't have many nights off, and when I do, I often cook for myself. But there's this restaurant near my house in Brooklyn called Rucola, which I've been to more than any other place in the world. My go-to order is crudo, their arugula salad, and whatever new pasta they're messing around with. It's a good order. This salad is as close as an homage can be to their arugula without trespassing into replication. I love the bright acidity of the dressing with the crunch of the radish. It's simple. It's easy to make. And it's delicious. But, I have to say, if you're in the neighborhood, just go to Rucola.

Preheat the oven to 350°F.

Make the croutons: In a bowl, toss the bread cubes with the olive oil and salt, pepper, and PX Spice to taste. Spread the cubes into an even layer on a sheet pan and bake, stirring once, until golden and crunchy, 15 to 20 minutes.

Assemble the salad: Place the radishes in a bowl of ice water to get them to curl up nicely, about 5 minutes. Remove from the water, drain, and pat dry.

In a large bowl, gently toss together half of the radishes, the kale, croutons, Pickled Shallots, and ½ to ⅔ cup of the dressing. Transfer to a salad bowl. Top with the remaining radishes, and enough Parmesan to cover the top of the salad.

RUCOLISH DRESSING

Makes 2 cups • Prep time: 10 minutes • Cook time: n/a

1 tablespoon grated lemon zest
⅓ cup fresh lemon juice
1 tablespoon celery seeds
2 tablespoons honey
1½ teaspoons mustard, homemade (see page 24) or Dijon
1½ teaspoons kosher salt
1½ teaspoons Roasted Garlic Puree (page 27)
½ cup finely grated Parmesan cheese
3 to 8 oil-packed anchovies
1 cup neutral oil

In a blender, combine the lemon zest, lemon juice, celery seeds, honey, mustard, salt, garlic puree, Parmesan, and the anchovies to taste, and process until smooth. With the blender running, slowly stream in the oil until fully emulsified. The dressing can be stored in an airtight container in the refrigerator for 3 to 4 days. Give a good shake before using.

Fennel Caesar Salad

Serves 4 to 6 • Prep time: 10 minutes • Cook time: 30 minutes

Fennel Oil and Dressing
1 cup neutral oil
1 cup fennel fronds, roughly chopped
1 tablespoon kosher salt
Rucolish Dressing (page 54)

Salad
2 fennel bulbs (1 pound total), quartered, cored, and shaved
2 cucumbers (1 pound), trimmed, cut into 3- to 4-inch lengths, julienned
2 green apples (1 pound), cored and julienned
Kosher salt
1½ cups Savory Granola (recipe follows)
Freshly grated Parmesan cheese, for serving

When people say they love a Caesar salad, what they're saying they love is the creamy anchovy lemony dressing. Romaine, the typical green for this salad, is great, but has nothing going on flavorwise. Fennel, on the other hand, now, fennel has character—a slightly licorice-y flavor that's crunchy at the bottom (the bulb) and herby up top (the fronds). This recipe uses both aspects of fennel, as well as swapping out the croutons (the second best part of a Caesar salad) for a delicious savory granola. More flavors; better crunch. The cheffiest thing about this recipe is also the easiest: the fennel oil. The bright pop of green from the oil is an impressive touch. Here I use the leftover tops and trimmings from the fennel to make the oil, but you can use any greens you have lying around—spinach, chives, basil, parsley. Whatever you use, make sure to cool it quickly, as that's how you maintain the brightness of the color.

Make the fennel oil: In a blender, combine the oil, fennel fronds, and salt and blend on high until smooth.

Preheat a small saucepan over medium heat. Transfer the oil mix to the hot pan, whisking constantly for 3 to 4 minutes. It should turn bright green.

Remove from the heat, pour into a cake pan (something wide and flat) and place in the fridge until cool. If you're really smart, you'll refrigerate the cake pan first or even freeze it—the faster you cool the oil, the brighter green it remains.

Make the dressing: Make the dressing as directed in the Rucolish Dressing recipe, but omit the celery seeds and use the fennel oil in place of the neutral oil called for. The dressing stays pretty green in the refrigerator for 1 day.

Assemble the salad: In a large bowl, mix together the shaved fennel, cucumbers, and apples. Gradually add 1½ cups of the dressing, tossing until everything is coated. Season to taste with salt.

To serve, transfer the salad to a prettier bowl and top generously with the granola. Finish with grated Parmesan and extra dressing on the side.

SAVORY GRANOLA

Makes 3 cups • Prep time: 5 minutes • Cook time: 25 minutes

½ cup pumpkin seeds
½ cup sunflower seeds
¼ cup white sesame seeds
¼ cup golden flaxseeds
¼ cup chia seeds
½ teaspoon kosher salt
¼ teaspoon freshly ground black pepper
2 cups freshly grated Parmesan cheese
1 tablespoon dried oregano
1 teaspoon Calabrian chile paste

Preheat the oven to 350°F.

Toss together all the ingredients on a sheet pan and spread into an even layer.

Bake until golden and fragrant, 15 to 20 minutes, stirring once.

Let cool completely, then break up into bite-size clusters. Store in an airtight container at room temperature for 3 months.

SOUPS & STEWS

Azemina's Beef and Barley Soup

Serves 4 to 6 • Prep time: 25 minutes • Cook time: 1 hour 30 minutes

- 1 pound beef chuck, small-diced (or just use ground beef)
- Kosher salt and freshly ground black pepper
- ½ cup all-purpose flour
- 4 tablespoons neutral oil, plus more as needed
- 1 small onion, small-diced
- 1 red bell pepper, small-diced
- 1 medium carrot, peeled and small-diced
- 3 garlic cloves, minced
- 1 tablespoon tomato paste
- 4 cups beef stock, broth, or water, plus more as needed
- 1 cup pearl barley
- 1 tablespoon chicken bouillon paste
- ½ teaspoon garlic powder
- ½ teaspoon paprika
- 2 tablespoons ajvar (optional)
- ¼ cup sliced fresh chives
- Very Easy Bread (page 178) or mashed potatoes, for serving

Everyone who struggled with addiction and is still here had someone who helped get them through. My someone was Azemina. She got me into rehab, and when the first one failed, she navigated the medical system to find another that was the right fit. (It allowed camping.) While I was in rehab, among other things, she remodeled my apartment so I had a new place to come home to. I owe her a debt I can never repay.

Part of Azemina's caregiving nature comes from her strong Albanian family, where this recipe was passed down from her grandmother to her mother to her. Whenever one of us is sick or homesick, this is her go-to. It's a simple soup, as befits a recipe passed down orally, with most of what work there is in the mise. To bring out the best flavor, she uses Vegeta, a Balkan bouillon with intense chicken flavor, and ajvar, a delicious and bright red pepper condiment. You can get it either in an Eastern European supermarket or from BalkanFresh.com.

Season the meat well with salt and pepper. Place the flour in a medium bowl, then toss the meat in the flour, shaking off any excess, and set aside.

In a large heavy-bottomed pot, heat 3 tablespoons of oil over medium heat. Working in batches, add the meat to the pot and cook, stirring occasionally and adding more oil as needed, until browned on all sides, 6 to 8 minutes. Transfer the meat to a plate and set aside.

Add 1 tablespoon of oil, the onion, bell pepper, carrot, and garlic to the pot and sweat for 5 minutes. Stir in the tomato paste and continue cooking, stirring occasionally, until the vegetables are softened and the tomato paste begins to caramelize, 3 to 5 minutes.

Add the stock and return the browned meat to the pot, increase the heat to high, and bring to a boil, scraping up the browned bits from the bottom of the pot. Add the barley. Stir in the bouillon, garlic powder, and paprika and season with a pinch of salt and pepper.

Cover the pot, reduce the heat to medium-low, and cook, stirring every 10 minutes or so, until the beef and barley are very tender and the stew has thickened, about 1 hour. Add more stock, 1 cup at a time, as it cooks if you notice it's getting really thick. When you feel you have about 10 minutes left, stir in the ajvar (if using). Season to taste with salt and pepper one more time.

Garnish with the chives. Serve immediately, with bread or mashed potatoes.

S.PELLEGRINO

SIRLOIN TIP
19/lb
Local, Pasture Raised
PB
SIRLOIN STRIP
24/lb
Local, Pasture Raised
PB
BAVETTE
25/lb
Local, Pasture Raised
PB
FLANK
25/lb
BONELESS STRIP
36/lb
Local, Pasture Raised
PB
BONE-IN NY STRIP
33/lb
Local, Pasture Raised
PB
30+ Day
43
/lb
Local, Pasture Raised
Grass Fed, Grain Finished
PB

Boy Scout Beef Stew

Serves 4 • Prep time: 25 minutes • Cook time: 2 hours

- 1½ pounds beef chuck, cut into 1-inch cubes
- Kosher salt and freshly ground black pepper
- ½ cup all-purpose flour
- 2 tablespoons vegetable oil, plus more as needed
- 2 medium Spanish onions, thinly sliced
- 3 garlic cloves, minced
- 2 tablespoons unsalted butter
- 6 cups beef stock, plus more as needed
- 2 carrots, peeled and cut crosswise on a bias into ¼-inch slices
- 2 russet potatoes, peeled and cut into ¼-inch dice
- 1 bunch thyme
- 1 bay leaf
- 12 cherry tomatoes, halved
- 1 cup frozen peas
- ¼ cup chopped fresh parsley, for garnish

I excelled as a chef because of the Boy Scouts, which I joined as a lanky, awkward seven-year-old. In the scouting world, there's a notion that once you're taught to do something, that thing will never be done for you again. If you are taught how to pitch a tent, no one will set up your tent for you. If you know how to build a fire, you can—and should—be building one yourself. As I found out years later, it is exactly the same in restaurants. When I first joined the Scouts, the dads would cook the beef stew for us. In time, they gave us a camping stove, a kit with unbreakable plates, salt, pepper, a can opener, and a can of beef stew to make for ourselves. Eventually, they gave us just the beef and potatoes and told us to figure it out. That's where I started to love cooking. I'm sure a lot of that love was for being in the woods with my dad, my brother, and the other Scouts. But a lot of it was feeling self-reliant, competent, and creative in the supportive (yet competitive) arena of scouting. And it all comes back to this delicious beef stew. Once you know it, teach it to all your friends.

Generously season the beef with salt and pepper. In a large bowl, toss the meat with the flour until well coated, shaking off any excess.

Heat a large cast-iron or heavy-bottomed pot over medium heat. Once hot, add the oil and heat until shimmering. Working in batches to avoid overcrowding, add the flour-dredged meat and sear the meat on all sides, stirring occasionally, until well browned, 5 to 6 minutes. Transfer it to a plate. Repeat with the remaining beef cubes, adding more oil as needed.

Once all the meat is browned, wipe the excess oil from the pot with paper towels and add the onions, garlic, and butter. Cover and allow to cook over medium heat, stirring once or twice, until the onions are softened, 5 to 7 minutes.

Return the meat to the pan, along with the beef stock, carrots, and potatoes. Increase the heat to high and bring to a boil. Once boiling, add the thyme sprigs and bay leaf, then season with salt and pepper. Cover, reduce the heat to medium, and allow the mixture to simmer for 1 hour, stirring frequently. Then remove the lid, add the cherry tomatoes, and cook until the liquid is reduced by half and the meat is very tender, another 45 to 60 minutes.

If at this time the stew looks good but the meat seems like it needs more time, add some more beef stock and let it reduce. Don't worry; this is a good thing. You are further concentrating the flavors.

Add the peas and let them cook for 5 minutes more.

Remove the stew from the heat and discard the thyme stems and bay leaf. Serve immediately, garnished with the parsley.

Irish Minestrone

Serves 4 • Prep time: 25 minutes • Cook time: 1 hour

2 tablespoons unsalted butter
2 tablespoons extra-virgin olive oil
2 medium yellow onions (1 pound 6 ounces), medium-diced
1 small purple-top turnip (6 ounces), peeled and medium-diced
1 carrot (6 ounces), peeled and medium-diced
1 russet potato (12 ounces), peeled and medium-diced
1 small sweet potato (9 ounces), peeled and medium-diced
2 garlic cloves, minced
8 cups chicken stock
1 sprig thyme
1 bay leaf
1 cup (5 ounces) diced ham (optional)
Kosher salt and freshly ground black pepper
1 cup fregola Sarda pasta
2 cups diced green cabbage
1 cup frozen peas
2 cups lightly packed fresh spinach
¼ cup fresh dill, chopped

I've never been a big reader (I'm dyslexic, have ADHD, and prefer to be outdoors), but when I started culinary school, I pored over *Le Guide Culinaire*, Auguste Escoffier's 1903 cookbook, like it was the latest Archie comic book. With over seven thousand recipes, the guide would be daunting for any culinary student, but I quickly realized there was a logic behind the French chef's recipes. Sometimes they're based on an ingredient. If he says something is Indienne, like Soufflé à l'Indienne or Poached Egg Indienne, there's curry or ginger in it. Sometimes it's based on color. If it is a Consommé à l'Irlandaise, you'll find the colors of the Irish flag in it: carrot (orange), turnip (white), and peas (green). I had found the decoder ring. This minestrone is, following Escoffierian logic, Irish: orange carrots; green peas and spinach; and white onions, potatoes, and pasta.

The most work you'll do for this recipe is the dice. You'll want to dice everything to the size of the smallest thing, in this case, about the size of a dime. Other than that, you're literally dumping everything into a pot and cooking.

In a large soup pot, heat the butter and olive oil over medium heat until the butter melts. Add the onions and sweat, stirring occasionally, until translucent, about 5 minutes.

Add the turnip, carrot, russet potato, sweet potato, garlic, stock, thyme, bay leaf, and ham (if using), and season generously with salt and pepper (less generously if you're using the ham). Bring to a simmer and cook until the vegetables are mostly tender, about 30 minutes.

Add the pasta and cabbage and simmer until the pasta is cooked through, about 15 minutes.

Check for seasoning, then add the frozen peas and spinach and cook until the spinach is wilted, another 2 minutes. Remove from the heat, discard the thyme stem and bay leaf, finish with the dill, and serve immediately.

Nonmonotonous Mulligatawny Soup

Serves 4 • Prep time: 35 minutes • Cook time: 40 minutes

- Twelve 1-ounce meatballs (optional; see page 151)
- 2 tablespoons extra-virgin olive oil, plus more as needed
- 1 medium yellow onion (8 ounces), small-diced
- 1 horse carrot (4 ounces; see below), peeled and small-diced
- 1 (2-inch) thumb fresh ginger, peeled and minced
- 3 garlic cloves, minced
- 1 tablespoon curry powder
- 1 tablespoon coriander seeds
- Kosher salt and freshly ground black pepper
- 1 apple (7 ounces), peeled, cored, and diced
- 6 cups chicken stock or water
- One 13.5-ounce can unsweetened coconut milk
- 1 large head broccoli (12 ounces), head cut into small florets and stalks peeled and small-diced
- 1 bunch spinach (10 ounces), tough stems removed, or 10 ounces baby kale

The first class you take in culinary school is Soups, Stocks, and Sauces. You learn how to make things like consommé, the French mother sauces, and an array of soups from lobster bisque to chicken noodle soup. To be honest, I always found soups boring. At least with a consommé, you're distilling chicken or veal or beef or mushrooms into its clear essence. With sauces, there's a genealogy and a logic there. Soup, on the other hand, always seemed like a bunch of blended ingredients, too lame to be alone. Mulligatawny was an outlier. This soup—which hails from South India, but is perhaps best known from *Seinfeld* (S7E6)—is infinitely variable. In Tamil, *mulligatawny* means "peppery water," but you don't even need pepper. (Here we use just a little as seasoning.) You can blend this soup as much or as little as you like to achieve your preferred texture. If you blend the entire soup, you'll want to serve it with something to break up the monotony, like apple chutney or curried meatballs. But if you want to serve the soup straight, I'd recommend blending only half of it and then mixing that back into the pot. That way you still get to keep some of the texture from the vegetables.

If adding meatballs, preheat the oven to 350°F.

In a large soup pot, heat the olive oil over medium heat until shimmering. Add the onion, carrot, ginger, garlic, curry powder, coriander seeds, and salt and pepper to taste. Cook, stirring occasionally, until softened and fragrant, 8 to 10 minutes.

Stir in the apple and cook until softened, another 5 minutes.

Add the stock and coconut milk, increase the heat to medium-high, and bring to a boil. Once boiling, reduce the heat to medium-low and allow the mixture to simmer, stirring occasionally, for 15 minutes.

Meanwhile, if adding the meatballs, place them on a sheet pan and drizzle the tops lightly with olive oil. Transfer to the oven and bake until cooked through, 10 to 12 minutes.

Add the broccoli to the soup pot and season with more salt and pepper. Return to a simmer and cook until the broccoli is almost tender, about 5 minutes. Stir in the spinach and cook until wilted, another 2 to 3 minutes.

Working in batches, carefully transfer the soup to a blender and blend on high until it's your preferred texture. The trick to blending is never to fill the blender more than halfway full so you let the motor do its thing. Adjust the seasoning if needed.

To serve, divide the soup equally into four bowls. Add 3 meatballs per bowl, if using, and serve immediately.

A HORSE CARROT IS ONE OF THOSE BIG CARROTS. THE SMALLER ONES WITH GREENS ATTACHED ARE CALLED SWEET BUNCH. YOU'LL NEVER NEED TO KNOW THIS.

SNACKS

Big Curd and Little Curd Ricotta

Making cheese seems daunting, difficult, and dangerous even. Mold! Time! Bacteria! But making ricotta is as simple as boiling milk. Add some acid, and thanks to the magic of chemistry, ricotta is yours. The combination of heat and acid forces the curds (the solids) and the whey (the liquids) to separate. Ladies and gentlemen, that's ricotta. And it takes less than 10 minutes to put together.

Now, depending on the type of acid you use, the nature of the curds will differ. Two chefs I worked with, Floyd Cardoz and Dan Barber, both preferred a larger, cheesier curd, which is made using buttermilk as the acid. I do, too, but I also love a creamier, softer version made with lemon juice as the acid.

BIG CURD RICOTTA

Makes 2 cups • Prep time: 5 minutes • Cook time: 15 minutes

4 cups whole milk
1 cup buttermilk
1 tablespoon kosher salt

In a small saucepan, bring the milk, buttermilk, and salt to a boil over medium heat. Reduce the heat to medium-low and allow to simmer, without stirring, until the curds and whey fully separate, about 8 minutes.

Set a fine sieve over a bowl. Gently ladle the curds and whey in and let the whey drain off for approximately 30 minutes.

LITTLE CURD RICOTTA

Makes 2 cups • Prep time: 5 minutes • Cook time: 15 minutes

4 cups whole milk
1 cup heavy cream
1 tablespoon kosher salt
¼ cup fresh lemon juice

In a small saucepan, bring the milk, cream, and salt to a boil over medium heat. Once boiling, add the lemon juice. Reduce the heat to medium-low and allow to simmer, whisking often, until the curds and whey fully separate, about 8 minutes.

Set a fine sieve over a bowl. Gently ladle the curds and whey in and let the whey drain off for 30 minutes.

Uses

- Drizzle with oilve oil and serve on a thick piece of sourdough
- Add to a tomato salad with stone fruit
- Dollop on a charcuterie plate
- Serve it in the pot it was made in, having guests scoop out the warm cheese from the milk
- Throw into a food processor with olive oil and blend until it's smooth. Use it as a spread.

Med
GoldSERIES
Med
6
4
Hi
Calories
120

An Ode to Popcorn and Its Many Variations

I was seven when *The Simpsons* came out and would watch the clock waiting for 7 p.m. when it came on to our local affiliate. Our whole family would watch together, and I was in charge of making the popcorn, the first time I was allowed to make something on my own. That's when I fell in love with butter; that's when I fell in love with cooking. Watching the butter melt in its saucepan, observing how it turned a hazelnut brown and filled the kitchen with a rich aroma. How if you let it get darker, that smell became acrid and then Dad would shout from the living room, "What's going on in there?" In a way, my career began with microwaved popcorn, a lot of salt, and melted butter. As I got older, I graduated to stovetop popcorn, which eventually convinced my parents I could grill chicken by myself, and the rest is history. Now I watch a lot of television, reruns exclusively, *The Simpsons* often, with a bowl of popcorn perched on my chest. It is what it is. My cooking skills have progressed since my first foray into popcorn, and I now have a stable of easy-to-make-but-nonetheless-cheffy variations, depending on my mood and what I have lying around.

Chicago-Style Popcorn
Garrett Popcorn shops are a Chicago institution whose mix of caramel and Cheddar popcorn is famous around the world. (I think. Maybe not.) It is, perhaps, the ultimate expression of popcorn.

Find a cute tin and toss together the Cheddar Popcorn (page 78) and Caramel Popcorn (page 78).

HOW TO MAKE POPCORN

My favorite way of making popcorn is melting the butter on the stove and using an air popper for the popcorn, stopping when the pops are a second or two apart. That way you get the lightest, airiest popcorn possible. If I'm feeling lazy, which I almost always am, I'll just microwave the popcorn, but will still melt the butter on the stove. (Microwaving butter is always messier than you think it'll be.) Stovetop popcorn works, too, but you'll likely end up with a few more unpopped kernels than with the air popper or in the microwave. When making one of the seasoned popcorns, I usually add one-third of the butter and a third of the salt first, toss, and repeat twice.

Air Popper Popcorn: Put ½ cup popcorn kernels in the machine and let it pop. Transfer the popcorn to a large bowl and toss with 2 tablespoons unsalted butter and ½ teaspoon kosher salt. Serve immediately. Makes 12 cups popcorn.

Microwave Popcorn: Microwave one 3.5-ounce bag of plain microwave popcorn following the package directions. Transfer the popcorn to a large bowl and toss with 2 tablespoons unsalted butter and ½ teaspoon kosher salt. Serve immediately. Makes 12 cups popcorn.

Stovetop Popcorn: In a large pot, heat 2 tablespoons neutral oil over medium heat until shimmering. Add ½ cup popcorn kernels, cover the pot, and shake constantly. After 3 minutes, remove the pot from the heat. Transfer the popcorn to a large bowl and toss with 2 tablespoons unsalted butter and ½ teaspoon kosher salt. Serve immediately. Makes 12 cups popcorn.

CHEDDAR POPCORN

If using any of the methods listed on page 77 for popping corn, omit the butter and salt.

Serves 5 (or 1, depending on level of sadness/hunger) • Prep time: n/a • Cook time: 10 minutes

12 cups popped popcorn
2 tablespoons unsalted butter, melted
½ teaspoon kosher salt
⅓ cup Cheddar powder (Medley Farms is pretty good)
Butter spray (optional)

Divide the popcorn into three bowls (this makes it easier to season evenly). Toss each portion of the popcorn with the butter and salt. Then sift the Cheddar cheese powder over each evenly, using butter spray to coat the kernels if needed for optimum stickage. It's best to do this while the popcorn is still warm. Combine the thirds in a large bowl and toss together.

CARAMEL POPCORN

If using any of the methods listed on page 77 for popping corn, omit the butter and salt.

Serves 5 (or 1, depending on level of sadness/hunger) • Prep time: 5 minutes • Cook time: 1 hour 5 minutes

8 tablespoons (4 ounces/1 stick) unsalted butter, plus more, softened, for the baking dish
12 cups popped popcorn
1 cup packed light brown sugar
¼ cup light corn syrup
½ teaspoon kosher salt
½ teaspoon baking soda
½ teaspoon pure vanilla extract

Preheat the oven to 250°F.

Butter a 9 by 13-inch baking dish and a spatula. Transfer the popcorn to the baking dish.

In a 1-quart saucepan, combine the butter, brown sugar, corn syrup, and salt. Bring the mixture to a boil over medium heat, stirring until the sugar dissolves and the butter incorporates. Allow to boil for 2 to 3 minutes, keeping a close eye on the mixture, occasionally swirling the pan, until darkened slightly and it begins to smell caramelized. Remove from the heat, then carefully whisk in the baking soda and vanilla (watch out, as it will bubble up a little vigorously at this point).

As soon as the foaming subsides, carefully but quickly drizzle the mixture over the popcorn, tossing to make sure all the kernels are evenly coated.

Transfer the popcorn to the oven and bake for 1 hour, stirring every 15 minutes or so.

Remove from the oven and let cool completely. Break up into bite-size pieces before serving.

THAI-FLAVORED CARAMEL CORN

If using any of the methods listed on page 77 for popping corn, omit the butter and salt.

Serves 5 (or 1, depending on level of sadness/hunger) • Prep time: 10 minutes • Cook time: 1 hour 5 minutes

8 tablespoons (4 ounces/1 stick) unsalted butter, plus more, softened, for the baking dish
12 cups popped popcorn
½ cup palm sugar (see below)
½ cup packed light brown sugar
¼ cup light corn syrup
1 teaspoon fish sauce
4 fresh makrut lime leaves
½ teaspoon baking soda
¼ cup bird's-eye chiles, each slit open
Grated zest of 2 limes (2½ teaspoons)
1 cup salted roasted peanuts
Neutral oil, for frying
5 shallots, sliced into thin rings on a mandoline

Preheat the oven to 250°F.

Butter an 11 by 13-inch baking dish or sheet tray. Transfer the popcorn to the baking dish.

In a medium saucepan, combine the butter, palm sugar, brown sugar, corn syrup, fish sauce, and lime leaves. Bring the mixture to a boil over medium heat, stirring until the sugar dissolves and the butter incorporates. Allow to boil for 2 to 3 minutes, occasionally swirling the pan, until the mixture has darkened slightly and it begins to smell caramelized. Remove from the heat, then whisk in the baking soda, chiles, lime zest, and peanuts.

As soon as the foaming subsides, carefully but quickly drizzle the mixture over the popcorn, tossing to make sure all the kernels are evenly coated.

Transfer the popcorn to the oven and cook for 1 hour, stirring every 15 minutes or so.

Line a plate with paper towels and place near the stove. In a small pot, combine 4 inches cold oil and the shallots and bring up to temperature over medium heat to 350°F. Fry, stirring often, until golden brown, about 10 minutes.

Immediately remove the shallots from the oil with a spider strainer or slotted spoon and spread onto the paper towels to dry and cool. You should have about 1 cup.

When the popcorn is done, remove it from the oven and stir in the fried shallots. Let cool completely, then break up into bite-size pieces before serving.

IF YOU DON'T HAVE PALM SUGAR, YOU CAN USE MORE PACKED LIGHT BROWN SUGAR INSTEAD.

DUCK FAT AND TOGARASHI POPCORN

If using any of the methods listed on page 77 for popping corn, omit the butter and salt.

Serves 5 (or 1, depending on level of sadness/hunger) • Prep time: n/a • Cook time: 5 minutes

- 12 cups popped popcorn
- 1 tablespoon unsalted butter
- 1 tablespoon duck fat (see Note)
- ½ teaspoon kosher salt
- 2 teaspoons togarashi, plus more as needed

Divide the popcorn into three bowls (this makes it easier to season evenly). In a saucepan, melt the butter and duck fat over medium heat. Slowly drizzle the fat mixture over each portion of popcorn while tossing it often. Season the popcorn with the salt and the togarashi according to your taste preference. Combine the thirds in a large bowl and toss together.

Note: If possible, try to obtain "seasoned" duck fat, which has been used to make duck confit a few times. This type of fat is richer in flavor, as the seasonings from the cured duck have infused into the fat. However, if seasoned duck fat isn't available, you can purchase regular duck fat on Amazon. But if you're going to go through the trouble of finding duck fat, it's worth making Duck Confit (recipe at right) with it a couple times to flavor the fat.

LEMON HERB POPCORN

If using any of the methods listed on page 77 for popping corn, omit the butter and salt.

Serves 5 (or 1, depending on level of sadness/hunger) • Prep time: Either no time or 15 minutes, depending on if you have the Lemon Herb Butter • Cook time: 2 minutes

- 12 cups popped popcorn
- ¼ cup Lemon Herb Butter (page 128)
- ½ teaspoon kosher salt

Add the popcorn to a large bowl. In a small saucepan, melt the Lemon Herb Butter over gentle heat. Drizzle a third of the butter and a third of the salt onto the popcorn and toss. Repeat twice more.

DUCK CONFIT

(a recipe for the sole purpose of seasoning duck fat for your popcorn)

Serves 4 • Cook time: 3 hours

- ½ cup kosher salt
- ½ teaspoon pink curing salt
- 2 tablespoons light brown sugar
- 2 sprigs thyme
- ¼ bunch parsley
- ¼ teaspoon freshly ground black pepper
- 3 garlic cloves
- A splash (½ teaspoon) brandy
- 4 duck legs
- 2 quarts duck fat

In a food processor, combine the kosher salt, curing salt, brown sugar, thyme, parsley, pepper, garlic, and brandy. Toss the mixture with the duck legs, then add the duck legs to a 9 by 13-inch pan, cover with plastic wrap, and let sit in the refrigerator for 24 hours.

When ready to cook, preheat the oven to 300°F.

Remove the legs from the cure, rinse, and pat dry. Place the legs in a baking dish deep enough that you can cover the legs with duck fat without worrying about spilling. In a saucepot, melt the duck fat over medium heat until liquefied. Pour over the duck legs, cover the baking dish with foil, and transfer to the oven.

Bake for 3 hours. Once finished, remove the duck legs, eat them, and reserve the fat for Duck Fat and Togarashi Popcorn (recipe at left) or other delicious things.

Chips and My Mom's Goop

Serves 4 • Prep time: 5 minutes • Cook time: 5 minutes • Inactive time: 1 hour

3 beef bouillon cubes
Two 8-ounce bricks Philadelphia cream cheese, at room temperature
¼ cup sour cream
1 small Spanish onion (12 ounces), small-diced
5 shakes of Worcestershire sauce (about ¼ teaspoon)
½ teaspoon kosher salt
1 bag as big as your *Weltschmerz* Lay's Potato Chips (see below)

This dip recipe holds a special place in my family's tradition, particularly the McGuires on my mother's side. Goop is a homemade version of a French onion soup dip, and we reserved it for special occasions or when company was over. (When it was just my immediate family, we used the actual French onion soup mix.) The McGuires had a humble upbringing—there were five kids and two adults, so they often had to ration their chips. To make a game of it, my grandmother and grandfather would sit on the two longer sides of a table and the kids would form a single-file line on one of the shorter sides. On one end was a bowl of chips; on the other, dip. Each child could take one chip, then walk to the far end and scoop up some goop. Then they could return and go again. That story has become a cherished part of our family tradition, just as this dish has become synonymous with memories of home. When I'm feeling homesick, I make it at my house where I eat it slowly, the McGuire way.

In a small saucepan, bring ⅓ cup water to a boil over high heat. Add the beef bouillon cubes, stir to dissolve, then remove from the heat and let cool completely.

In a stand mixer fitted with the paddle (or in a bowl with a hand beater), combine the cream cheese, sour cream, onion, Worcestershire sauce, salt, and about 5 tablespoons of the cooled bouillon liquid. (If you prefer a thinner dip, you can add more bouillon liquid as desired.)

Refrigerate for at least 1 hour before serving with the potato chips.

FEELING HEALTHY? USE RAW VEGGIES INSTEAD OF CHIPS.
(BUT I ALWAYS USE CHIPS.)

Dueling Chicken Wings

Serves 4 • Prep time: 15 minutes • Cook time: 45 minutes

24 chicken wings (about 2½ pounds), split into flats and drummies
Canola oil
Kosher salt
½ cup Heirloom Pepper Hot Sauce (page 25)
4 tablespoons unsalted butter, cubed
¼ cup Milu Chili Crisp
¼ cup thinly sliced green onions
2 cups assorted pickles (see How to Pickle Some Things, page 38)

Doing something two ways always seems fancier than doing it one way, but it is rarely twice the work. (From what I hear from parents, though, it's the exact opposite with kids. Which is why I have none.) These dueling chicken wings are a good example. The base chicken wings are the same, but there are two different types of spice: a tang from the fermented hot sauce and more chunky umami from the chili crisp. I serve these during Cubs v. Yankees games. You can—and probably should—bake the wings ahead of time. That way, you don't need to fry them as long while your guests wait and you miss the game.

Preheat the oven to 350°F.

Pat the wings dry, drizzle them lightly with oil, and season them with salt. Place the wings in an even layer on a sheet pan and bake for 25 minutes. Remove from the oven and set aside.

Set a wire rack in a sheet pan and have near the stove. Fill a Dutch oven about halfway with oil and heat over medium heat until it reaches 350°F.

Working in batches of 6, depending on the size of the pot, fry the wings, stirring occasionally, until golden brown, 6 to 8 minutes. Transfer to the wire rack to drain. Adjust the heat as needed to keep the temperature as close to 350°F as possible, allowing the oil to return to temperature between batches.

Meanwhile, in a small saucepan, warm the hot sauce over medium heat. Slowly add cubes of butter, swirling the pan until melted into the sauce. Keep warm over low heat.

While the wings are still hot, toss half of them in the hot sauce. Toss the other half with the chili crisp. Divide into opposing teams. Garnish with the sliced green onions and serve with assorted pickles.

Harbison Fondue with Garlic Crostini

Serves 4 to 6 as an appetizer (or 2 to 3 if you're from the Midwest) • Prep time: 10 minutes • Cook time: 25 to 30 minutes

Garlic Crostini

- ½ baguette, cut into ⅛-inch-thick slices (stale is fine)
- ⅓ cup extra-virgin olive oil
- PX Spice (page 19) or kosher salt and freshly ground black pepper
- 3 garlic cloves, peeled but whole

Harbison Fondue

- One 9-ounce wheel Harbison or Brie (around 5 inches in diameter)
- 1 bunch Pickled Radishes (page 39), cut in half
- 1 Honeycrisp apple, cored and medium-diced
- 1 sprig rosemary (optional: see below)

The cheese course is the fine-dining world's greatest trick. It feels fancy to be presented with a little cart bearing wheels of obscure cheeses. It feels luxurious as you bask in the recitation of their origin, nodding as if you know what's going on. And most important, it feels triumphant as you let the richness, sharpness, sweetness, funkiness, *chees*iness melt into your mouth. You are winning at life. And yet it all takes almost no work—just slicing and spieling.

So when you put even a mote of effort into the cheese course, it hits. For years, we used this Harbison Fondue as our cheese course at Olmsted. Here is the spiel we used as we served it: "Harbison is a soft cow's milk cheese made by our friends at Jasper Hill Farm in Greensboro, Vermont. It's wrapped in spruce bark and finished for 6 to 8 weeks. It has a bloomy rind and woodsy notes." (I checked and it's fine for you to say "our friends" too, even if you don't know Andy and Matteo, the founders of the farm.) All you do is cut off the top of it and pop it in the oven until it emerges gooey. We served it with garlic crostini—crispy garlic-rubbed toast—and a bunch of delicious cheese-to-mouth conveyors, aka things to dip.

Make the garlic crostini: Preheat the oven to 350°F.

Lay the sliced bread on a baking sheet and generously drizzle with the olive oil. Season with PX Spice. Bake until they turn golden brown and crisp (the bread should almost fry in the oil) 18 to 20 minutes.

Remove from the oven and rub one side of each slice three times with a clove of garlic while still warm. Leave the oven on for the cheese.

Make the Harbison Fondue: Cut off the top layer of the cheese rind, just to expose the inside. Place on a sheet pan and bake until it softens, about 5 minutes.

Once softened, switch the oven setting to broil. Move the pan to about 6 inches below the heating element and broil until golden brown and bubbling, 2 to 4 minutes.

Transfer the cheese to a platter and surround the cheese with the Pickled Radishes, apple, crostini, and if using, the rosemary sprig. Serve with fondue forks if you've got them!

CAREFULLY TORCH THE ROSEMARY AND ADD IT TO THE PLATTER. THE AROMA COMPLEMENTS THE SPRUCE-WRAPPED HARBISON.

Nuts, but the Fun Kind

Makes 3 cups or so • Prep time: n/a • Cook time: 20 to 30 minutes

½ cup almonds
½ cup cashews
½ cup pecans
½ cup pumpkin seeds
2 tablespoons extra-virgin olive oil
1 tablespoon kosher salt
2 tablespoons sugar
2 tablespoons curry powder
1 cup dried cherries

I do zero entertaining now, but when I was married, we used to have people over all the time. I always made these nuts ahead of time so I could have something nice to serve when people arrived while buying myself about 30 more minutes of hiding in the kitchen. You don't have to use this exact mix of nuts—I often just used whatever nuts we had lying around in the apartment. In fact, the most important thing about this recipe actually isn't the nuts, it's overcoming social anxiety. Just kidding; the most important thing is to use high-quality dried cherries.

Preheat the oven to 350°F.

In a medium bowl, combine the almonds, cashews, pecans, pumpkin seeds, olive oil, 1 tablespoon water, the salt, sugar, and curry powder. Spread evenly on a sheet pan and bake until fragrant, 20 to 30 minutes, stirring halfway.

Remove from the oven, sprinkle with the dried cherries, toss, and serve warm.

Store in a sealed container in a cool, dry place for a month or so.

Rehab Nachos

Serves 4 • Prep time: 10 minutes • Cook time: 15 minutes

Tortilla Chips

About ten 6-inch corn or flour tortillas
Canola oil, for frying
Kosher salt

Cheese Sauce

1 cup heavy cream
4 cups grated sharp Cheddar cheese (1 pound)
¼ cup roughly chopped pickled jalapeños

Assembly

1½ cups shredded beef (optional; see Notes), such as Boy Scout Beef Stew (page 63) or Homey Braised Beef Short Rib (page 141)
⅓ cup sour cream
2 Fresno chiles, thinly sliced (⅓ cup)
2 green onions, thinly sliced (⅓ cup)
⅓ cup fresh cilantro, torn or very roughly chopped

If you think that going to rehab will get you ripped—like I did, the first time I went—I have bad news for you: Rehab centers, like hospitals, schools, and prisons, rely on unhealthy industrial food. Why? It's cheaper. Duh. The first time I was in rehab, I lived off hot dogs, burgers, nachos, and reruns of *Dexter*. Now, whenever I watch *Dexter*, I have a Pavlovian response and yearn for those nachos again. This version is, well, better. I use a trick I learned at Per Se from Matt Orlando, who was a sous at the time. He made mac and cheese by combining equal parts cream and shredded cheese, which made a super-delicious and easy cheese sauce, akin to queso. I like to add pickled jalapeños to my sauce because I like a little spice, and I find that the vinegar in the jalapeños prevents the cheese from becoming grainy.

This recipe is delicious and easy, but does not reheat well. So just give in to your basest impulses and finish the whole thing, bingeing *Dexter* until it's 2 a.m. and you fall asleep with queso caked to your lips. Or, you know, share it with friends if you have them.

Make the tortilla chips: Preheat the oven to 350°F. Cut the tortillas into quarters.

Set a wire rack in a sheet pan and have near the stove. Fill a Dutch oven with 4 inches oil and heat over medium-high heat until it reaches 350°F.

Working in batches, fry the tortilla quarters, stirring occasionally, until pale golden and crisp, about 2 minutes. Drain on the wire rack and sprinkle with salt while hot. Adjust the heat as needed to keep the temperature as close to 350°F as possible, allowing the oil to return to temperature between batches.

Make the cheese sauce: In a medium saucepan, bring the heavy cream to a boil over medium heat, stirring frequently. Once boiling, reduce the heat to low and add the cheese and jalapeños. Whisk until the cheese is melted and well incorporated (see Notes). Remove from the heat and let sit about 5 minutes, until thickened.

Assemble the nachos: Place the chips in a small cake pan or baking dish. Drizzle with the cheese sauce and top with the beef (if using). Bake for about 5 minutes to heat through. Remove from the oven and garnish with dollops of sour cream, Fresno chile rings, green onions, and cilantro.

Notes

– When you shred the beef, toss with any leftover juices to keep it moist.

– A stick blender is the best thing to use here, since you want to incorporate the vinegary pickling liquid into the cheese so the sauce doesn't get grainy. But look, if this is the only time you're going to use that stick blender, a whisk is totally fine.

VEGGIES

Carrot Crepes

Makes 10 crepes • Prep time: 35 minutes • Cook time: 35 minutes

Carrot Butter
1 cup carrot juice
2 tablespoons heavy cream
8 ounces (2 sticks) unsalted butter, chilled and diced
Kosher salt
2 tablespoons minced fresh chives

Carrot Crepes
1 cup all-purpose flour
1 teaspoon kosher salt
3 large eggs
2 tablespoons unsalted butter, melted and cooled slightly
1 cup carrot juice (see below)
Cooking spray, for the pan

The carrot crepe put Olmsted on the map. In his 2016 two-star review, *New York Times* critic Pete Wells called it a "strange and fascinating appetizer that got into my head and now I want it again." When I opened Olmsted, at the end of May, the Union Square Greenmarket, which everyone thinks will be verdant then, was a ghost town. I was, at the time, super serious and rigid about seasonality. If strawberries weren't at the market, there would be no strawberries. Yadda, yadda, yadda. So, for the opening menu, I wrote down a list made up of two columns: On the left side were fruits and vegetables I knew I could get like apples, carrots, etc., and on the right side, I wrote a list of proteins I knew I wanted to use. Then I just connected items on the two lists with dotted lines based on what I thought would complement each other. Carrots and littleneck clams were paired up last like the final two kids in gym class. It was my challenge to make them a winning team for our opening menu. Thanks to the sweetness of the carrots and the brininess of the clams (and their jus), I think I did.

This recipe omits the clams (who's going to make a strange and fascinating appetizer at home?), but you still get the bright Oompa Loompa–colored crepe, which tastes like buttered carrots but eats like silk.

Make the carrot butter: In a small saucepan, simmer the carrot juice over medium heat until only 2 tablespoons of liquid are left. Stir in the cream and reduce by half.

Reduce the heat to low and slowly whisk in the butter. Once the butter is melted, remove from the heat and use a stick blender (or transfer to a stand blender) to blend on low for just a few seconds to thicken the sauce. Season with salt to taste and add the chives.

Make the crepes: In a large bowl, combine the flour and salt. In a medium bowl, combine the eggs, butter, and carrot juice. Whisk the liquid mixture into the dry ingredients.

Spray a nonstick skillet with cooking spray and wipe out with a paper towel. Place over low heat and add ¼ cup of batter to the pan. Swirl the batter until the bottom of the pan is coated in a thin layer. After about 2 minutes, flip the crepe using an offset spatula and leave on the heat for 30 seconds more, then remove. Fold the crepe into quarters to stack them (it makes them easier to handle and minimizes the risk of rippage). Repeat with the remaining batter, spraying and wiping the pan again as needed to keep the crepes from sticking.

Coat the folded crepes with the butter sauce, and serve.

WANT A RED CREPE? A YELLOW CREPE?
REPLACE THE CARROT JUICE WITH BEET
OR SWEET POTATO JUICE.

GoldSERIES
Med
Lo
4
6

Med
GoldSERIES

Cauliflower Okonomiyaki

Makes 3 pancakes • Prep time: 30 minutes • Cook time: 5 minutes

1 head cauliflower (2 pounds)
Kosher salt
½ cup potato starch
4 large eggs, beaten
3 garlic cloves, minced (1 tablespoon)
1 bunch green onions, white and green parts separated, thinly sliced
2 inches fresh ginger, peeled and minced (about 1 tablespoon)
3 tablespoons neutral oil
¼ cup Yuzu Mayo (page 27)
¼ cup Tonkatsu Sauce (recipe below)
¼ cup toasted hazelnuts, roughly chopped
1 teaspoon black sesame seeds, for garnish

I'm a Francophile, always have been. But whenever I go out to a bistro, I eat the steak and the fries and the baguette and the butter, and invariably I'm always too full for the *tête de veau ravigote*, the frog legs persillade, and the leek mayonnaise, and curse myself for lacking self-control. What if that restraint was built in? What if you could have the French flavor profiles but served as yakitori, a genre of small Japanese foods served on a skewer, so that you can try a little bit of everything? That was my impetus for opening Maison Yaki in 2019: dishes with French flavors in Japanese form.

Even though the restaurant was known for its skewers, by far the most popular dish was our cauliflower okonomiyaki. Cauliflower with hazelnuts is a classic French flavor combination, and it's often served with brown butter and truffles. Okonomiyaki is a traditional Japanese savory pancake made with cabbage and pork, cooked on a teppan, a hot steel plate. The nuttiness of the hazelnuts wingmans the caramelization of the cauliflower, and it's all topped off with an umami-filled homemade tonkatsu sauce.

Preheat the oven to 350°F.

Remove the leaves from the cauliflower and cut the head into quarters. Using a mandoline, shave the cauliflower into thin slices. Transfer the slices to a colander set over a bowl and give them a good shake to let the small bits fall out. Set these little cauliflower bits aside for use as a garnish later.

In a medium pot, combine one-quarter of the sliced cauliflower with enough cold water to cover it. (Reserve the remaining shaved cauliflower for later.) Season with salt, bring to a simmer over medium-high heat, and cook until the water is gone and the cauliflower is tender. Drain the cauliflower and puree until smooth. (An immersion blender is helpful here; a regular blender will do, though.)

In a large bowl, combine the cauliflower puree with the rest of the sliced cauliflower, the potato starch, eggs, garlic, the whites of the green onion, the ginger, and 1 tablespoon salt, mixing until incorporated into a batter.

In a 6-inch ovenproof cast-iron skillet, heat 1 tablespoon of the oil over medium heat until shimmering. Add one-third of the batter (about 1 cup) to the pan, patting it down so it occupies the entire area of the pan. Let the batter cook for about 1 minute on the stove, until golden. Then transfer the pan to the oven for 5 minutes. Remove the pan from the oven and flip the pancake. Cook for another minute, then remove from the pan.

Repeat with the remaining thirds of the batter and another 1 tablespoon of oil to make each pancake.

Whisk 2 teaspoons water into the Yuzu Mayo to loosen it up for a better drizzle.

Top the okonomiyaki with the Tonkatsu Sauce, Yuzu Mayo, toasted hazelnuts, sliced green parts of the green onions, and the reserved crumbled bits of the raw cauliflower. Garnish with the sesame seeds.

TONKATSU SAUCE

Makes 1¼ cups • Prep time: 5 minutes • Cook time: n/a

1 cup ketchup
¼ cup soy sauce
2 teaspoons Worcestershire sauce

In a small bowl, whisk together the ketchup, soy sauce, and Worcestershire sauce. Store excess in an airtight container in the refrigerator.

Delicata Squash Vase

Serves 4 • Prep time: 25 minutes • Cook time: 40 minutes

2 delicata squash (12 ounces each)
1 tablespoon extra-virgin olive oil, plus more for drizzling
Kosher salt and freshly ground black pepper
One 3-ounce package thinly sliced prosciutto
8 tablespoons (4 ounces/1 stick) unsalted butter
1 bunch sage, leaves picked
1 cup Little Curd Ricotta (page 72)
2 cups packed baby kale
1 small head (4 ounces) radicchio (see Note), leaves separated and torn into smaller pieces
3 tablespoons balsamic vinegar
1 Bartlett (or other) pear (7 ounces), cored and cut lengthwise into ⅛-inch-thick slices

The most important thing to know about a delicata squash vase is that it's a vase, rhymes with Oz, not vase, rhymes with maze. I insisted on this pronunciation with such stickleriness when we first opened Olmsted that now my staff corrects me when my vowels open too wide and my Chicago accent peeks out. The second, and more important, thing to know is how easy a squash vase is to make, and how impressive it can be. This is thanks to the squash itself. Delicata have thin skins, which means you can eat the entire thing (and easily hurt its feelings). There's no fussy skin-peeling to be done (or snobby judgment of those who leave the skin behind). The idea of the squash as a vessel came from searching for something that a) looks soigné and b) is really easy to execute. At Olmsted, with its small kitchen and high hopes, this was key. There, we filled the squash about one-quarter of the way up with ricotta, which we then used as a sort of putty into which we arranged some bitter leaves, some sweet pears, and some crispy prosciutto. But the beauty of this vessel is that you can fill it with anything you'd like. As you cut into the steamed squash, the whole thing yields, falling apart on the plate into an instant warm salad.

Preheat the oven to 350°F.

Trim the heads and tails from the delicata squash, leaving flat surfaces on both ends. Then halve each squash crosswise—making cups, not canoes—and remove the seeds. Season with a drizzle of olive oil and salt and pepper.

Place the squash, cut-side down, on one half of a sheet pan. Lay out the prosciutto on the other half of the pan. Transfer to the oven.

Bake until the squash is fork-tender and the prosciutto has crisped up, about 10 minutes. (If the squash takes a little longer, just remove the prosciutto so it doesn't become too crispy.) Remove from the oven and let the squash cool for about 10 minutes.

Meanwhile, line a plate with paper towels and have near the stove. In a sauté pan, melt the butter over medium heat. Once the foaming subsides, add the sage leaves. (They'll pop and hiss when the water meets the fat.) When the popping stops, pick out the sage leaves, lay on the paper towels, and season with salt.

Allow the butter to cool slightly and then pour it into a food processor (or a bowl). Add the ricotta and blend (or just whisk) together. Season with salt and pepper and set aside.

In a large bowl, dress the kale and radicchio leaves with the balsamic vinegar, olive oil, salt, and pepper.

To assemble, fill each squash vase one-quarter of the way up with ricotta. Make a bouquet with the radicchio and kale leaves, pear slices, prosciutto, and sage leaves in each vase and serve immediately.

Note: You can use endive here instead if it's easier to get. If using endive, cut off the bottom, separate the leaves and halve them lengthwise.

Purple-Top Turnip Parm-less Parm

Serves 2 to 3 • Prep time: 20 minutes • Cook time: 2 hours

2 purple-top turnips (about 1 pound total), washed and scrubbed
2 tablespoons extra-virgin olive oil
Kosher salt and freshly ground black pepper
½ cup all-purpose flour
2 large eggs
1 cup panko bread crumbs, finely ground
Canola oil, for frying
2 cups Marinara Sauce (recipe follows)
1 teaspoon dried oregano
1 teaspoon PX Spice (page 19)
2 balls fresh burrata, halved
1 ploosh of fresh basil (see Note)

Note: A ploosh is what I always called a bunch of fresh herbs like chervil, parsley, or basil with their leaves cut small. I guess it should be pluche or plushe, like a velvety pillow, but I'm American, dammit, and I'm spelling it ploosh, like it sounds, rhymes with Koosh.

My time at Blue Hill made me think about vegetables in a creative way. Because they were such a focus in Dan Barber's kitchens, by the time I left I was convinced that they could be stars of any dish. Why not in a Parm? Think about it: A Parm can be chicken, veal, eggplant, shrimp . . . whatever. It's what is on top that counts—gooey melted mozz under a sharper armor of Parm, sitting atop something with a crispy coat, all bathed in the glory of marinara. So, why not a root vegetable? Rutabaga, celery root, turnip—just roast it off, bread it, and fry it into a Parm for an anytime vegetarian entrée.

Preheat the oven to 300°F.

Coat the turnips with the olive oil and season with salt and pepper. Tightly wrap each one in foil and bake until fork-tender, about 1½ hours. Remove from the oven, but leave the oven on and increase the temperature to 375°F.

Set up a dredging station in 3 bowls: Add the flour to a shallow bowl. Beat the eggs in a second bowl. Add the panko to a third.

Trim the top and the tail of the cooked turnips and cut them into roughly ½-inch-thick crosswise "steaks" (3 to 4 per turnip). Season the turnips again with salt and pepper, then toss each steak in the flour, tapping off excess. Dip each steak into the egg, allowing excess to drip back into the bowl. Then dredge in the panko, pressing gently so the crumbs adhere to both sides.

Line a baking sheet with paper towels and have near the stove. Pour ½ inch canola oil into a sauté pan and heat over medium heat until shimmering. Add the turnips and cook, flipping once, until GBD (golden brown delicious) on both sides, 5 to 6 minutes (adjust the heat as needed). Set aside on the paper towels to drain.

Season the marinara with the oregano, PX Spice, and a pinch of salt. Add the sauce to the bottom of a 6-inch cast-iron pan or a glass baking dish. Top with the turnips. Arrange the burrata halves over the top. Season again lightly with salt and pepper and transfer to the oven.

Bake until the cheese is melted and just beginning to brown, 20 to 25 minutes. Remove from the oven, top with basil leaves, and serve immediately.

MARINARA SAUCE

Marinara sauce is good for all of the big Ps: Pizza, Pasta, Parm.

Makes 3½ cups • Prep time: 10 minutes • Cook time: 40 minutes

2 tablespoons extra-virgin olive oil
1 Spanish onion, thinly sliced
¼ cup white wine
One 28-ounce can crushed tomatoes
1 tablespoon Roasted Garlic Puree (page 27)
Kosher salt and PX Spice (page 19)

In a medium saucepan, heat the olive oil over medium heat. Add the onion and cook, stirring occasionally, until softened, 5 to 6 minutes.

Add the wine and cook until reduced by half, 1 to 2 minutes. Stir in the tomatoes and garlic puree and season with salt and PX Spice to taste. Bring to a boil, then reduce to medium-low heat and simmer until thickened slightly, about 30 minutes.

Puree in a blender until mostly smooth with some chunks remaining.

Heirloom Tomato Schnitzel

Serves 2 • Prep time: 15 minutes • Cook time: 10 minutes

¾ cup all-purpose flour
3 large eggs, whisked
2 large heirloom tomatoes or large beefsteaks (1½ pounds total)
Kosher salt and freshly ground black pepper
2 tablespoons extra-virgin olive oil
4 tablespoons (2 ounces) unsalted butter
1 cup diced shallots (2 large shallots)
2 tablespoons thinly sliced fresh chives

In the summer, everybody puts peaches and heirloom tomatoes on a plate with a ball of burrata on top of it. Great. And while that's delicious, I didn't want to do the same thing as everyone else. In addition, I wanted an heirloom tomato dish, not just a salad—it had to be warm and it had to have caramelization. I learned that grilling the tomatoes turned them to mush but, after further experimentation, I found that coating the slices with egg and flour before frying them produced the crispiness I desired while not overly manipulating the product. Plus, as has been well documented in this book, I'll fry literally anything.

Place ½ cup of the flour in a large bowl. Slowly whisk the eggs into the flour until mostly smooth.

Cut off the top and bottom of each tomato to create 2 flat sides. Then cut both tomatoes in half horizontally, creating 4 hockey pucks roughly ¾ inch thick. Season with salt and pepper on both sides. Dredge each puck in the remaining ¼ cup of flour, then dip it in the egg batter, scraping most of the batter off using the side of the bowl.

In a large sauté pan, heat the olive oil over medium heat until shimmering. Add the tomatoes and sauté, flipping once, until both sides are golden brown, 2 to 3 minutes per side. Transfer the tomatoes to serving plates and drain off the oil from the pan.

Add the butter and shallots to the same pan and sauté until the butter has melted and the shallots have softened, about 2 minutes. Spoon over the tomatoes. Top with the chives.

Med
Lo
GoldSERIES

Butter-Roasted Oyster Mushrooms

Serves 4 as a side • Prep time: 5 minutes • Cook time: 30 minutes

- 4 tablespoons (2 ounces) unsalted butter, at room temperature
- 1 teaspoon yuzu koshō
- 2 pounds oyster mushrooms, on the stem if possible (2 large bundles)
- Kosher salt and freshly ground black pepper
- 3 tablespoons Tonkatsu Sauce (page 96)
- ¼ cup Yuzu Mayo (page 27)
- 1 teaspoon white sesame seeds
- 1 teaspoon black sesame seeds
- ⅛ teaspoon crushed sanshō pepper
- ¼ cup sliced green onions, green parts only

The world is more divided now than it ever has been, but we can all agree that crispy things are good to eat. Mushrooms rarely get crispy, as they are, by nature, almost as logged with water as they are rich with umami. But oyster mushrooms, with their large oyster-shaped caps and decurrent gills, are an exception. Expose these babies to high enough heat and the edges get crisp like a fall day. The basic technique here—coating them in butter and shoving them in a pan, stems attached—helps the mushrooms retain their shape and their texture. I like to finish them with yuzu koshō mayo and tonkatsu sauce, but feel free to improvise. It might be nice to add to a hollandaise, or toss with a store-bought pesto, or perhaps some of Floyd Cardoz's spice blends from Burlap & Barrel.

Preheat the oven to 400°F.

In a small bowl, combine the butter and yuzu koshō. Brush the butter onto the mushrooms, getting into all the nooks and crannies. Season with salt and black pepper.

Place the mushrooms in a pan just big enough to fit them snugly, so they stay upright, and transfer to the oven.

Bake until the mushrooms are tender and the edges turn crispy, 20 to 30 minutes.

Carefully remove the mushrooms from the oven and, using a knife or a pair of scissors, cut away the stem, liberating the mushroom caps. Toss the mushrooms in the Tonkatsu Sauce.

To serve, smear the Yuzu Mayo onto a plate. Top with the tonkatsu-enrobed mushrooms, sprinkle with the sesame seeds and sanshō pepper, and finish with the green parts of the green onions.

Summer Squash Som Tum

Serves 4 to 6 as a side • Prep time: 20 minutes • Cook time: 25 minutes

Thai Crunchy Topping (page 111; see Note)
1 yellow summer squash, top trimmed
1 medium zucchini, top trimmed
1 medium red onion
1 cup 1-inch pieces trimmed green beans
1 cup cherry tomatoes, halved
1 medium cucumber, diced
1 recipe Thai Dressing (page 111; see Note)
½ bunch fresh shiso leaves, cut into nickel-size pieces
½ bunch fresh mint leaves, cut into nickel-size pieces
½ bunch fresh basil leaves, cut into nickel-size pieces
1 Fresno chile, thinly sliced

Som tum is a Thai salad that's usually made with julienned green papaya, but I've discovered that zucchini and summer squash work well as substitutes. What elevates this from a run-of-the-mill squash salad into something brighter and more fun is the umami-filled textured crunch of the Thai topping.

Make the crunchy topping as directed and set aside.

Using the medium-size teeth of a mandoline, julienne the squash and zucchini lengthwise into long noodles.

Set up a bowl of ice water. Peel and trim the top and bottom of the red onion. Cut into quarters and then, using the toothless blade of the mandoline, thinly shave the onion into the ice water. When ready to use, drain.

Bring a small pot of water to a boil over high heat. Add the green beans, letting them blanch for 4 minutes. Remove and run under cold water to stop the cooking.

In a large bowl, toss together the onion, yellow squash, zucchini, tomatoes, cucumber, and green beans. Toss with the Thai Dressing. Transfer to a nice serving bowl and top with the shiso, mint, basil, chile, and the crunchy topping.

Note: Want to make it vegetarian or vegan? Substitute dark soy sauce for the fish sauce in the dressing and omit the dried shrimp from the crunchy topping.

Hard-Won Mandoline Wisdom

Techniquewise, or rather, technologywise, you're going to want to use a mandoline for this recipe. (Yeah, you could julienne with a knife, but it's drudgery.) So, let's go over some basics:

When starting out using a mandoline, wear either two sets of latex gloves on the cutting hand or those yellow dishwashing gloves. If you nick yourself, it'll just catch the gloves.

That final little bit of whatever you're slicing is never worth the blood. Don't get too close. (Good advice for relationships, too.)

Continued

Starfish
Brazilian Pepper
$12/Lb
HuskCherry
$16/Lb
BE
EST.

THAI CRUNCHY TOPPING

Makes 2 cups • Prep time: 5 minutes • Cook time: 15 minutes

6 medium shallots
Neutral oil, for frying
½ cup dried shrimp
½ cup toasted cashews

Preheat the oven to 350°F.

Peel the shallots and then slice into thin rings on a mandoline using the toothless blade.

Line a plate with paper towels and have near the stove. In a small pot, combine the shallots and 4 inches cold oil and bring up to temperature over medium heat to 350°F. Fry, stirring often, until golden brown, about 10 minutes. Use a spider strainer or slotted spoon to remove and spread on the paper towels to drain.

Meanwhile, grind the dried shrimp in a coffee grinder or a spice grinder until they form a powder.

In a food processor, combine the shrimp and toasted cashews and pulse the mixture until blended into coarse crumbs. Toss with the crispy shallots.

THAI DRESSING

Use this dressing in the Summer Squash Som Tum (page 108), and if you want, use it to make Thai Mayonnaise (page 26), which I just thought of now.

Makes 1 cup • Prep time: 5 minutes • Cook time: n/a

¼ cup fish sauce
⅓ cup fresh lime juice (2 to 3 limes)
¼ cup packed light brown sugar (or palm sugar if you can find it)
2 garlic cloves, peeled but whole
½ Fresno chile, stemmed and seeded
1 tablespoon sliced lemongrass, outer leaves removed
1 fresh makrut lime leaf, optional

In a blender, combine the fish sauce, lime juice, brown sugar, garlic, chile, lemongrass, and lime leaf (if using) and blend on high until smooth. Store airtight in the refrigerator for up to 1 week.

Romano Bean Sofrito

Serves 4 as a side • Prep time: 15 minutes • Cook time: 1 hour 50 minutes

- 4 beefsteak tomatoes (2½ pounds) or one 14.5-ounce can crushed tomatoes (whatever, doesn't matter)
- ½ cup extra-virgin olive oil
- 1 large Spanish onion, thinly sliced
- 5 garlic cloves, minced
- 1 tablespoon dried oregano
- 1½ teaspoons chile flakes
- 1 cup white wine
- 1 pound Romano beans, trimmed and cut on a bias into 2-inch strips (to resemble penne)
- 1 teaspoon red wine vinegar
- Kosher salt and freshly ground black pepper

When I was first working at Thomas Keller's Per Se, the kitchen was run by Jonathan Benno, the chef de cuisine. Benno had a real simple style, based in clean Italian cuisine, unlike the more complicated dishes of many traditional fine-dining chefs. Since I was on the fish station and actually had to do all my own prep, I was always glad when it was Benno who wrote the menu. Less work for me. It also helped teach me that there's no correlation between the level of complexity and the level of deliciousness of a recipe. Simple doesn't automatically mean better, but certainly neither does complex.

This Romano bean sofrito is very much inspired by my time with Benno. It strips down a sofrito—traditionally a mix of celery, carrots, garlic, and onion—to its very core (in this case onion and garlic), adds tomato, and then uses that as a flavorful cooking medium for the Romano beans. Benno used to do this with tripe, but who's cooking tripe at home and who really wants to? These snappy sweet beans offer a lighter, more vegetal flavor. I cut the beans into penne-size pieces and treat them like a gluten-free pasta. Serve as a side with a piece of fish.

Preheat the oven to 350°F.

If using fresh tomatoes, blend them in a food processor or grate on the large holes of a box grater (see below).

In a large ovenproof sauté pan, heat the olive oil over low heat until shimmering. Add the onion, garlic, oregano, and chile flakes and cook, stirring occasionally, until the onion is softened, about 8 minutes.

Add the wine, increase the heat to medium-high, and bring to a simmer. Cook until reduced by half, 5 to 7 minutes.

Add the beans and tomatoes and bring to a boil. Once boiling, add the vinegar, season with salt and pepper (heavy on both), and stir to combine. Transfer to the oven.

Bake until the liquid has thickened slightly and the beans are very tender, about 60 minutes; the time will depend on how wet the tomatoes are.

IF YOU GRATE THE TOMATOES, YOU'LL GET A MORE EVEN TEXTURE.

POULTRY

Calabrian Chile and Red Onion Chicken Schnitzel

Serves 4 • Prep time: 20 minutes • Cook time: 15 minutes

Chicken Schnitzel
2 boneless, skinless chicken breasts
½ cup all-purpose flour
3 large eggs, whisked
2 tablespoons extra-virgin olive oil
Kosher salt and freshly ground black pepper

Calabrian Chile Sauce
3 tablespoons unsalted butter
½ large red onion, thinly sliced
Kosher salt and freshly ground black pepper
2 teaspoons Calabrian chile paste
3 tablespoons mayonnaise (see below)
2 tablespoons chopped fresh parsley
2 teaspoons fresh lemon juice

A lot of schnitzel is served with cream, capers, and lemons in a piccata-like sauce. It's delicious, but what I usually have lying around is not that. I typically have Calabrian chile paste, which never goes bad, usually a lonely onion rolling around my vegetable drawer, and mayonnaise. Lots of mayonnaise. (I am, after all, from the Midwest.) This schnitzel recipe uses all those lonely pantry pickings to make a simple but very flavorful meal. The basic frying technique—the egg and flour wash—I picked up at Per Se. I decided to use the same pan to both fry and make the sauce because I hate doing dishes.

Preheat the oven to 350°F.

Make the chicken schnitzel: Slice the chicken breasts in half horizontally to create 4 thin cutlets. Set aside.

Place the flour in a large bowl. Slowly whisk the eggs into the flour until the batter is mostly smooth.

In a medium sauté pan, heat the olive oil over medium heat until shimmering. Season the chicken cutlets with salt and pepper. Dip each cutlet into the batter, then scrape most of it off using the side of a bowl. You want just a thin shell. (You'll make a doughnut around it if it is too thick.)

Place 2 chicken cutlets in the pan and sauté until golden brown on both sides, about 2 minutes a side. Repeat with the remaining cutlets, then transfer to a baking sheet and keep warm in the oven.

Make the Calabrian chile sauce: Dump out the oil from the sauté pan. Add the butter and red onion, season with salt and pepper, and return to medium heat. Cook until the butter melts, tossing with the onion. Add the Calabrian chile paste and ¾ cup water, swirling the pan to emulsify the fat into the water. Let it reduce until glossy, 1 to 2 minutes. Reduce the heat to low and stir in the mayonnaise, parsley, and lemon juice until emulsified.

Working in batches, place each chicken schnitzel in the sauce, flipping it, 30 seconds a side to coat. Season once more with salt and pepper. Serve immediately.

FANCY CHEFS WOULD USE CAULIFLOWER OR ONION PUREE IN THE SAUCE BUT I USE MAYONNAISE AND IT'S PRETTY GOOD. YOU DON'T HAVE TO USE IT IF IT GROSSES YOU OUT.

Continued

BUFFALO CHICKEN SCHNITZEL SANDWICHES

Makes 4 sandwiches • Prep time: 15 minutes • Cook time: 15 minutes

4 pieces chicken schnitzel (see page 116)
2 tablespoons extra-virgin olive oil
2 baguettes, ends trimmed and split horizontally in half
1 cup mayonnaise
¼ cup Heirloom Pepper Hot Sauce (page 25)
1 head lettuce, rinsed and dried
¼ medium red onion, sliced
1 tomato, thinly sliced
½ cup Pickled Celery (page 39)
½ cup crumbled blue cheese

Preheat oven to 350°F. Once heated, warm the chicken schnitzel for 15 minutes.

In a large skillet, heat the oil over medium heat. Add the split baguettes and toast. (You could also do this in the oven. If the bread is fresh, no need to toast it.)

In a small bowl, whisk together the mayo and hot sauce.

Build the sandwiches by laying open the baguettes and evenly spreading the spicy mayo on both sides of each.

Then, starting from the bottom, add the lettuce, red onion, tomato, and Pickled Celery. Add the chicken and crumble the blue cheese over top. Close the sandwich and enjoy it, considering what other times you've felt yourself a leftover.

Garlicky Braised Chicken with Tostitos Salsa

Serves 4 • Prep time: 20 minutes • Cook time: 1 hour 20 minutes

- 1½ pounds boneless, skinless chicken breasts or thighs (about 2 breasts or 4 to 6 thighs), cut into 1-inch chunks
- 3 tablespoons all-purpose Vegeta stock powder or chicken bouillon powder
- Freshly ground black pepper and kosher salt
- ½ cup all-purpose flour
- 3 tablespoons extra-virgin olive oil, plus more as needed
- 1 medium yellow onion (8 ounces), thinly sliced
- 1 head garlic, minced (¼ cup)
- 4 cups water
- 3 cups cooked or drained canned chickpeas (from two 15-ounce cans)
- 1 cup Tostitos salsa (see below), or more as desired
- 2 cups packed stemmed kale leaves, chiffonade-cut

Braising, a cooking method halfway between roasting and stewing, should be a model for all relationships: forgiving, low-maintenance, long-term, and reparable. Once you master the braise, you can braise anything and the world itself becomes a one-pot wonder. The most important aspect of braising is trying to time it so that the cooking medium—stock, water, a bunch of leftover salsa—doesn't reduce too much before the meat is done. Tender meat and a nappé sauce (thick enough to coat the back of a spoon) are the goals, and you might have to add more water as you go to make sure the sauce doesn't reduce too soon. (The opposite is hardly a problem. It's very difficult to overcook something braised.) At the end, you'll end up here with a delicious all-in-one meal that goes great over rice or on its own.

Season the chicken with 2 tablespoons of the Vegeta and ¼ teaspoon pepper. Place the flour in a medium bowl and toss the chicken in the flour until coated, shaking off any excess flour.

In a large cast-iron skillet, heat the olive oil over medium heat until shimmering. Working in two batches, add the chicken to the pan in an even layer and cook, turning the chunks occasionally, until golden brown all over (see below), 3 to 5 minutes. If necessary, replenish with more oil as needed. Once the chicken is seared, transfer it to a plate.

Add the onion and garlic to the skillet, cover, and allow them to sweat until softened, about 5 minutes.

Return the chicken and any accumulated juices to the pan, along with the water, the chickpeas, salsa, and the remaining 1 tablespoon Vegeta. Season lightly with salt and pepper.

Set over medium-low heat and simmer, stirring occasionally, until the liquid is thick and saucy and the chicken is very tender, 40 to 45 minutes, adding more water as needed to keep the chicken partially submerged. Just before you turn off the heat, stir in the kale.

Check for seasoning and serve immediately.

GO TO THE FRIDGE, FIND ALL THE LEFTOVER SALSA YOU HAVE AND ADD IT TO THE POT. HELL, YOU CAN EVEN USE VAGUELY SALSA-LIKE THINGS LIKE TOMATO SAUCE.

NO ONE HAS TIME TO SEAR EVERY SIDE OF AN IRREGULAR CHUNK. AIM FOR TWO.

NON-ALCOHOLIC BREW
ATHLETIC
BREWING

Chicken Fingers and French Fries

Serves 4 to 6 • Prep time: 40 minutes • Cook time: 40 minutes • Inactive time: 1 hour 30 minutes

- 6 russet potatoes (about 3 pounds total)
- ¼ cup distilled white vinegar
- Neutral oil, for frying
- 1 cup all-purpose flour
- 6 large eggs
- 4 cups panko bread crumbs
- 4 boneless, skinless chicken breasts (about 2 pounds), cut into ½-inch-thick strips
- ¼ cup Baxtrom Spice (page 19)
- Kosher salt and freshly ground black pepper
- Too much ketchup

OK BUY A TEMP GUN, A THERMOMETER THAT USES INFRARED WITHOUT CONTACT. IT MAKES HEATING OIL MUCH EASIER THAN USING A CANDY THERMOMETER OR GUESSING.

Chicken fingers get classified as kid food because . . . why? They're easy to eat, easy to make, and delicious? They're universally beloved, crispy, and tender? Because kids like repetition and you can eat chicken fingers for lunch, as I do often, and dinner, as I also do often, on the same day? Sometimes it happens that I eat so many frozen chicken fingers and fries watching reruns of *Seinfeld,* while my dog, Spud, watches me watching, eating errant crumbs and the occasional fallen fry, that when it comes time for dinner and I want to continue my frozen-chicken-finger-and-fry marathon, I can't because I've eaten them all, so I have to make a recipe on the fly from scratch using my Baxtrom Spice to elevate them slightly.

Really the only note for this recipe applies to all frying, and that is to watch your oil temperature. Anything less than 350°F is going to take too long and yield an overcooked product. (The exception is intentionally underdone fries, but you'd refry them anyway.) Work in batches so as not to lower the temperature too much and let the oil come back up to temp before adding another batch.

Preheat the oven to 200°F.

Using a mandoline, slice the potatoes lengthwise into ⅛-inch-thick planks then, using a knife, cut them into ⅛-inch-thick strips. Place in a large bowl and cover completely with cold water. Let sit for 15 minutes, then drain and cover with fresh water again. Let sit for another 15 minutes, drain again, then cover with water and add the vinegar. Allow to sit for at least 1 hour or up to 24 hours.

Meanwhile, set a wire rack in a sheet pan and have near the stove. Fill a Dutch oven with 4 inches oil and heat over medium-high heat to 300°F (see note at left).

Drain the potatoes well and pat dry. Working in batches—around three batches—add to the oil and fry, stirring a few times, until mostly cooked through but not developing any color, about 5 minutes. Lift from the oil using a spider strainer or slotted spoon and let drain on the wire rack. Adjust the heat as needed to keep the temperature as close to 300°F as possible, allowing the oil to return to temperature between batches.

When all the potatoes have had their first round of frying, increase the heat to high and bring the oil up to 350°F. Set another wire rack in a sheet pan and have near the stove.

Set up a dredging station in 3 shallow bowls: Add the flour to the first bowl. Break and beat the eggs in a second bowl. Add the panko to a third. Season the chicken strips with the Baxtrom Spice and lightly with salt and pepper. Toss the chicken in the flour. Then, working in batches, dip each strip into the eggs, allowing any excess to drip back into the bowl, then add to the panko, pressing gently to make the crumbs stick, and then place into the oil. Fry the strips until golden and cooked through, 3 to 5 minutes.

Transfer the chicken to the wire rack and keep warm in the oven.

Meanwhile allow the oil to return to 350°F and fry the fries a second time until golden and crispy, 4 to 6 minutes. Drain on another wire rack and season with salt to taste while they're hot.

Serve with too much ketchup in some noninfantalizing way or, if you're like me (I yearn for the purity of childhood), an infantalizing one.

Grilled Chicken Paillard with House Salad

Serves 4 • Prep time: 20 minutes • Cook time: 10 minutes

4 boneless, skinless chicken breasts
3 tablespoons plus 4 teaspoons extra-virgin olive oil
Grated zest and juice of 1 lemon
1 teaspoon chile flakes
Kosher salt and freshly ground black pepper
1 carrot (4 ounces), peeled and thinly sliced on a bias
1 cucumber (8 ounces), sliced as thinly as possible on a bias
¼ medium red onion, thinly sliced
1 tablespoon distilled white vinegar
½ cup ajvar (I like Mama's)
½ cup whole-milk Greek yogurt
1 head Bibb lettuce, cleaned and leaves separated

Uses

Before I forget, here are a few things I use ajvar for:

- Add it to mac and cheese
- Toss it with pasta or scrambled eggs
- Use as a sandwich spread
- Stir into a stew
- Add to pimento cheese

Many cultures have their own roasted pepper spread. Muhamarra in the Middle East. Peperonata in Italy. Poivronade in the South of France. Ajvar is the Balkan version: tangy, smoky, creamy, and fruity. I buy mine on Amazon. My favorite is Mama's Ajvar, which is made from slowly roasted vegetables and hand-peeled peppers from Macedonia. The subtle smokiness goes really well with chicken paillard, which is really just chicken pounded thinly and quickly grilled. (This French cooking technique was originally developed for veal but works just as well with chicken.) Here I use it in a tangy yogurt sauce that goes underneath the chicken. Whenever I eat chicken, I feel like I'm making healthy choices with my life. This super-simple house salad—which you can, and should, use as an accompaniment to other recipes, too—is just more evidence that I'm nailing it. Right? I am, right? I don't know. The salad is good, though.

Lay a chicken breast in front of you. Starting on the fat side that has an indent, work a knife blade horizontally through the breast, leaving about ½ inch on the far side connected. Peel the breast open. It'll look like a dead chicken butterfly, or a book. You want the breast to lie flat. If it doesn't, you might then take the knife and deepen the incision. But don't do it all at once. You're not that good. Repeat with all the chicken breasts.

Working one at a time, place a chicken breast in a 1-gallon zip-seal plastic bag with 1 teaspoon of olive oil. Using a rolling pin, a meat mallet, or something heavy, pound the chicken breasts to an even ¼-inch thickness.

Place the chicken in a shallow dish. Add the lemon zest, lemon juice, chile flakes, and 2 tablespoons of the olive oil. Season with salt and pepper. Let marinate at room temperature for 10 minutes or so while you prep the rest of the ingredients.

In a bowl, combine the carrot, cucumber, onion, vinegar, and the remaining 1 tablespoon of olive oil. Season with salt and pepper and set aside.

Heat a grill pan over medium-high heat until smoking. Grill the chicken breasts, working in batches if needed, 3 to 4 minutes a side (but see below), until cooked through.

Meanwhile, in a medium bowl, combine the ajvar and yogurt, whisking until well mixed.

Once all the chicken has been grilled, add the lettuce to the lightly dressed vegetables and toss to combine.

To serve, place about ¼ cup of the ajvar sauce at the bottom of a plate. Pat the bottom of the plate like a baby's bottom to gently spread the sauce. Top with a grilled chicken paillard, then garnish with the salad.

MORE IMPORTANT THAN GETTING GOOD GRILL MARKS ON BOTH SIDES IS HAVING GREAT GRILL MARKS ON ONE SIDE, WHICH MEANS MAYBE YOU'RE COOKING ONE SIDE FOR SIX MINUTES AND THE BACK SIDE FOR TWO MINUTES. GRILLING ISN'T LIKE JOINT CUSTODY: EACH SIDE DOESN'T NEED TO GET EQUAL TIME.

Lemon Herb Chicken Kyiv

Serves 4 • Prep time: 35 minutes • Cook time: 25 minutes • Inactive time: 5 hours

2 boneless, skinless chicken breasts (12 ounces each)
4 tablespoons plus 4 teaspoons extra-virgin olive oil
Lemon Herb Butter (recipe follows), refrigerated until firm
1 cup all-purpose flour
3 large eggs
2 cups plain dried bread crumbs
Canola oil, for frying
Kosher salt and freshly ground black pepper

When I was growing up, everyone was busy. Mom. Dad. Me. My sister and brother. In high school, the first one home after practice or work would turn on the oven and throw something in it. Often it was frozen. Pizza, pizza rolls, Salisbury steak, pu pu platter, whatever. If I knew I would be eating alone, I'd dig out the elusive frozen Chicken Kyiv. There was never enough for a family, so this was a solitary pleasure. Chicken Kyiv is basically chicken breast wrapped around a stick of garlic butter, which is then breaded and baked. When you cut open the chicken, the butter oozes out. It was my idea of heaven.

This version brings me back to those glory days of my youth, albeit with some more finesse. The trick is to nail the timing. You need butter cold enough not to melt out right away, but not so cold it remains a frozen block. Freezing the chicken-wrapped butter for 3 hours gets the balance right. Usually, I'll make two of these at a time—one for now and one to freeze—and I'll serve it either with a mess of arugula, topped with olive oil and lemon (1 cup of arugula per Kyiv), or just double down on the decadence and serve with mashed potatoes.

Carefully cut the chicken breasts horizontally, yielding four thinner pieces.

Working one at a time, place a chicken breast in a 1-gallon zip-seal plastic bag with 1 teaspoon of olive oil. Using a rolling pin, a meat mallet, or something heavy, pound the chicken breasts to an even ¼-inch thickness.

Place 1 log of butter on one of the shorter edges of a flattened chicken breast and roll it away from you until the chicken encases the butter. Wrap tightly in plastic wrap. Continue with the other three, then transfer to a plate and freeze for 3 hours until very firm.

When ready to cook, set up a dredging station in 3 shallow bowls: Place the flour in one bowl. Beat together the eggs in the second bowl. And spread bread crumbs in the third.

Remove the chicken from the freezer. Bread the chicken thusly: Dip in flour, then egg, then flour, then egg (shaking off the excess each time). Finally add to the bread crumbs, patting to adhere. Return the chicken to the plate and refrigerate until the butter is no longer frozen solid, about 2 hours.

When ready to cook, preheat the oven to 325°F.

Pour a generous amount of oil into a large deep cast-iron skillet and heat over medium heat until 350°F. Set a wire rack in a sheet pan and have near the stove.

Remove the chicken from the refrigerator. Add to the oil and cook, rotating occasionally, until golden brown all over, 4 to 5 minutes total. Transfer to the wire rack to drain (see Note). Season with salt and pepper.

Transfer the sheet pan to the oven and bake until cooked through, 16 to 18 minutes. The chicken is usually done by the time the butter begins to ooze out. But another way to test is to take a paring knife, a cake tester, or a thermometer and stick it into the chicken diagonally. Pull it out and place it on your wrist. If it hurts, it's probably done. This is how we do it in restaurants. Get over it.

Note: At this point, if you want to freeze them for later, let them cool to room temperature, wrap them in plastic or in a zip-seal plastic bag, and freeze. When you want to eat them, pull them out 12 hours before and let thaw in the refrigerator. Then cook on a wire rack in a sheet pan in a 325°F oven for 20 minutes.

Continued

LEMON HERB BUTTER

This herb butter is also great on the Lemon Herb Popcorn (page 79), for the Calabrian Chile and Red Onion Chicken Schnitzel (page 116), or spread on the Very Easy Bread (page 178).

Makes four 2-ounce logs • Cook time: n/a • Inactive time: 1 hour

8 ounces (2 sticks) unsalted butter, at room temperature
Grated zest of 1 lemon (1 packed teaspoon)
¼ cup chopped fresh herbs, such as dill, parsley, or chives
1½ teaspoons kosher salt
Freshly ground black pepper

In a medium bowl, whisk together the butter, lemon zest, herbs, salt, and pepper to taste until smooth. (Or blitz together in a food processor.) Divide the mixture into 4 equal portions. Place each on a sheet of plastic wrap and form into a log about the width of a quarter and 3 inches long. Wrap in the plastic and refrigerate until firm, at least 1 hour. (These logs can last a few days in the fridge and a few months in the freezer.)

Roasted Chicken Crown with Pickled Cherries, Fennel, and Favas

Serves 4 • Prep time: 30 minutes • Cook time: 50 minutes

1 cup House Pickling Liquid (page 38), made with red wine vinegar (see Notes)
1 pint sweet Bing cherries
2 chicken crowns (about 1¾ pounds each; see Notes)
Kosher salt and freshly ground black pepper
4 tablespoons neutral oil
2 cups shelled fresh fava beans
4 tablespoons (2 ounces) unsalted butter
3 garlic cloves, smashed, skin on
1 sprig thyme
2 bunches young fennel (1¼ pounds with tops; 3 to 4 bulbs per bunch)
2 tablespoons extra-virgin olive oil

A chicken crown (see Notes) looks like a cute little avian football, a chicken pin cushion. But in addition to looking cool, it's also practical: Cooking on the crown is actually half the time and half the effort of roasting a whole chicken, because you don't have to worry about the legs cooking at different rates than the breasts. Because it's easy and showy, chicken crown is a dinner party hit—you bring it out to the table and everyone always oohs and aahs. Then you return to the kitchen to carve it, which, incidentally, gives the bird time to rest. At Per Se, where this was a mainstay, we had a whole routine around the chicken crown. When it was ready to go out, you'd call out, "Fly the bird." When it came back, and was ready to be carved, the person bringing it back to the kitchen would call out, "Bird Bacharach." (For young people, Burt Bacharach was a famous American composer and singer, perhaps best known for "What's New Pussycat?") As for the accompaniment, this combo is pure late spring/peak summer, when fennel, fava, and cherries are in abundance at the Greenmarket. In winter, I'd replace the fennel and fava with Brussels sprouts and turnips (but would still hunt for cherries to pickle, as their tartness is key to the flavor).

Preheat the oven to 350°F.

In a small pot, heat the pickling liquid over medium heat until simmering. (Or just microwave it for 1 minute on high.)

Smoosh the cherries with the palm of your hand to open them. Remove the pits and then add the fruit to a medium bowl. Pour the hot pickling liquid over them and let stand while you continue with the recipe.

Season the chicken crowns on both sides with salt and pepper. In a large ovenproof sauté pan, heat 2 tablespoons of the neutral oil over medium-high heat until shimmering. Add one of the chicken crowns, skin-side down, and sear for about 3 minutes, or until browned. Remove the chicken and set aside. Allow the pan to return to temperature, then repeat with the second chicken crown. Return the resting chicken crown to the pan, flipping both crowns breast-side up (it's okay if it's a little crowded) and transfer to the oven.

Bake until cooked through, 30 to 40 minutes, depending on the size of the chicken crown.

Meanwhile, bring a medium pot of heavily salted water to a boil over medium-high heat. Add the fava beans and cook for 4 minutes. Drain and let cool slightly. When cool enough to handle, squeeze the skins until the inner bean pops out.

Remove the chicken from the oven (see Notes), but leave the oven on. Add 2 tablespoons of the butter, the garlic, and thyme to the pan, set over low heat, and baste for a few minutes. Remove from the heat and let rest for about 10 minutes.

Meanwhile, trim the tops from the fennel, reserving the fronds for garnish. Trim the base of the fennel and then cut into quarters; shave off the cores and discard.

Continued

In another ovenproof sauté pan large enough to fit all the fennel in an even layer, heat the remaining 2 tablespoons of butter and 2 tablespoons of neutral oil over medium heat. Once the butter melts, add the fennel and season with salt and pepper. Sauté until golden brown, about 5 minutes, then flip it and place in the oven for 5 minutes.

Add the warm fava beans and fennel to the bowl with the pickled cherries and toss to combine. Check for seasoning. Add the olive oil to make a quick vinaigrette. (The pickling liquid provides the acid.)

Carve the chicken breast off the bone, then cut into thick slices.

Serve with the salad, topped with fennel fronds, if you desire.

Notes:

- A chicken crown is a cut of chicken with the full breast (both sides) on the bone with the skin on and tucked beneath to make a neat compact shape. You can either ask for a crown from your butcher or make your own by removing the wings, drumsticks, and thighs from a chicken.
- Because the cherries are red, it makes sense to use the red vinegar pickling liquid from, like, a romantic standpoint. But it doesn't actually matter which vinegar you use.
- Fresh fava beans are protected by both a pod and thick skin, both of which need to be removed before eating. At super-fancy places, you would peel the favas before they're blanched. But it's infinitely easier to blanch them still in the skin, which then slips off when gently pressed. So do that.

SHIT! I UNDERCOOKED THE CHICKEN. DOESN'T MATTER. SOMETIMES CHICKEN IS BETTER A LITTLE UNDERCOOKED AT THIS POINT. IF YOU DID, GET THAT DELICIOUS GARLIC THYME BUTTER RIPPING HOT. ONCE HOT, TURN OFF THE HEAT AND ADD THE CHICKEN BREAST, UNDERCOOKED PART DOWN. THE HEAT OF THE BUTTER WILL COOK THE BREAST BUT NOT OVERCOOK IT.

Chicken Kebabs with Sautéed Spinach and Mushroom Rice

Serves 4 • Prep time: 20 minutes • Cook time: 25 minutes

Chicken Kebabs

½ cup whole-milk Greek yogurt
1½ teaspoons curry powder
3 pounds boneless, skinless chicken breasts (about 4) or thighs (8 to 12), cut into 1-inch chunks
Kosher salt and freshly ground black pepper
Neutral oil, for the pan
Lemon wedge, for garnish

Mushroom Rice

1 tablespoon neutral oil
4 cups diced cleaned portobello mushrooms
1 Spanish onion, diced
3 garlic cloves, grated
1 tablespoon ground coriander
Kosher salt and freshly ground black pepper
1 tablespoon unsalted butter
1 cup brown rice

Sautéed Spinach

1 tablespoon olive oil
1 tablespoon unsalted butter
8 cups spinach
1 Garlic Fork (see page 53)
Kosher salt and freshly ground black pepper
Lemon wedge

If you, like me, eat grilled chicken breast twice a day every single day seven days a week, your thirst for novelty might trump your innate laziness. No, I do not like extra steps. Yes, these steps—cutting the chicken into chunks so the marinade can better penetrate them while simultaneously exposing more surface area for the almighty Maillard reaction—are worth it. The marinade is easy to make and quick acting.

Prepare the chicken kebabs: In a medium bowl, whisk together the yogurt and curry powder. Season the chicken pieces with salt and pepper and add to the yogurt marinade, tossing to coat. Let stand at room temperature for about 10 minutes.

Meanwhile, start the mushroom rice: In a large sauté pan, heat the oil over medium heat until shimmering. Add the mushrooms and let them sweat for 10 minutes.

Add the onions, garlic, coriander, salt, pepper, butter, and rice and mix well. Cover tightly with a lid and reduce the heat to medium-low. Cook until rice is done, about 20 minutes.

Make the sautéed spinach: Heat the olive oil and butter in a separate large sauté pan over medium-high heat. Add half of the spinach, then stir it down until it wilts using the garlic fork. Add the second half of the spinach. Once it cooks down, season with salt, pepper, and a squeeze of lemon and remove from the heat.

Meanwhile, preheat the oven to 350°F and heat a grill pan or outdoor grill to medium-high heat. Brush the pan or grill grates lightly with oil. Skewer the chicken on metal or presoaked wooden skewers. Grill the skewers on both sides, 4 to 5 minutes a side, until the internal temperature reaches 165°F. You can pop them in the oven to keep warm and cook through if needed. Serve some chicken, some rice, and some spinach on a plate with a wedge of lemon.

WHY DO I EAT CHICKEN SO MUCH? I'M VERY EXTREME. I'M A BLACK AND WHITE THINKER. CHICKEN IS HEALTHY SO I WILL ONLY EAT CHICKEN. ALSO, I'M CHEAP. ALSO LITHIUM MAKES ME VERY SNACKY SO I TRY TO FILL UP ON HEALTHY THINGS SO I DON'T JUST SNACK ON POTATO CHIPS ALL DAY.

Smoked Duck Pastrami

Serves 4 to 6 • Prep time: 15 minutes • Cook time: 3 hours • Inactive time: 48 hours

- 2 boneless duck breasts (1½ pounds total), cleaned and trimmed
- 1 quart Everything Brine (page 37), cooled
- 7 tablespoons Pastrami Rub (recipe follows)
- 1 cup hickory or cherrywood chips, plus more as needed

How to Clean a Duck Breast: Duck breasts usually arrive with a thin skein of silver sinew and skin that sits on a layer of fat. You typically want to protect the lean breast meat from direct heat with the fat, and you want the fat to be even in thickness. Place the duck skin-side down and remove the sinew. Use a paring knife to trim the skin where it extends beyond the meat. Even out the lumpy bits of fat on all sides to make sure it is about the uniform thickness.

Chefs love duck because it's like highbrow chicken. And we love brining and curing and smoking, because it makes us feel like food alchemists. Brining, curing, and smoking duck? It's like playing with all your favorite toys. When we were forced to close Olmsted in March 2020, we were left with a fridge full of ducks. Thinking fast, we used the brine reserved for our beef pastrami to preserve the ducks and then, three days later, smoked them in our smoker out back. Once we reopened, the ducks made it onto the menu. This recipe simplifies that process, but lets you have all those heroic chef moments; and the best part is the moist, tender, and rich pastrami that comes out at the end.

Place the duck breasts in a large zip-seal plastic bag and pour the brine over the top. Seal and place in the refrigerator for 48 hours. (Make sure the duck is fully submerged in the brine. You may need to place it in a pan and put something on top of it to weigh it down.)

When ready to cook, remove the duck from the brine and pat dry. Spread the Pastrami Rub out on a plate and roll the breasts in the rub, patting to make sure as much of each breast is as encrusted as possible.

In a smoker: Set your smoker to 165°F and smoke the duck with the wood chips for 2 hours.

In the oven: Preheat the oven to 250°F.

Place the duck in a deep 9 by 13-inch pan and transfer to the oven.

Cook until the duck reaches an internal temperature of 165°F, about 2 hours.

Add the wood chips to a dry sauté pan on the stove over high heat (or under a broiler) until smoking, about 5 minutes. Yeah, you're gonna start a fire. But it's a controlled one. So . . . no big deal? Add the smoldering wood chips to a small ovenproof bowl and place in the pan along with the duck. Cover tightly with foil.

Cook for another hour or so, relighting the wood chips every 15 minutes.

To serve: Serve hot, cold, or at room temperature. It's so damn good it doesn't matter.

PASTRAMI RUB

Makes 1¾ cups

- ¾ cup freshly ground black pepper
- ⅔ cup ground coriander
- ⅓ cup ground mustard seeds

In a small bowl, combine the pepper, coriander, and mustard seeds. Store in an airtight container for, like, a really long time.

Uses

You can use Pastrami Rub like any other spice mix, adding it to a braise, to a soup, to a roast. It's delicious. You could technically put it on popcorn. Technically you can put anything on popcorn.

MEATS

A Good Clean NY Strip with Chanterelles and Shishitos

Serves 4 • Prep time: 15 minutes • Cook time: 20 minutes

4 New York strip steaks (8 ounces each), each about 1 inch thick
Extra-virgin olive oil
Kosher salt
PX Spice (page 19)
1 pound shishito peppers
Juice of ½ lemon, plus more as needed
2 tablespoons good butter
3 garlic cloves, smashed but skin on
1 pound chanterelles, stems trimmed, cut in half (leave whole if small)
Flaky salt, to garnish

When you shell out $40 for chanterelle mushrooms or God knows how much for a nice steak, you're not looking to cover them up. This is a super-simple recipe with only three main ingredients, which means you need to think about each ingredient carefully and use the highest-quality ingredients you can. Each main ingredient—the steak, the mushrooms, and the shishitos—calls for a different method of preparation. The steak needs the high heat for the char, the shishitos need blistering to release more flavor, and the chanterelles, with their delicate, almost apricot-like flavor, need a more gentle approach. By softening them in garlic-infused butter you preserve their subtlety, which you just paid for through the nose. Don't waste lipstick on a pig when the pig is already beautiful, you know? The reward is a dinner that comes together in minutes but tastes wonderful.

Preheat a large cast-iron grill pan over high heat.

Pat the steaks dry, drizzle lightly with olive oil, and season generously with salt and PX Spice.

Place the steaks in the pan, grilling roughly 4 minutes per side. (You might have to work in batches so as not to overcrowd the pan.) Transfer the steaks to a cutting board and let rest for 10 minutes, flipping them halfway through the resting process. (In my head, this allows the juices to fall to the bottom, then flip to return the other way. Who knows if that's true?)

Toss the shishitos with a drizzle of olive oil and season with salt and PX Spice. Add to the hot pan you used for the steak and grill, tossing once, until slightly blistered, 4 to 5 minutes, working in batches if necessary. Remove to a plate and squeeze lemon juice over the peppers.

Meanwhile, in a large sauté pan, melt the butter over medium heat. Add the garlic and then the chanterelles, season with salt and PX Spice, and cook, stirring occasionally, until softened, about 6 minutes. (No need for color here.)

Remove from the heat and toss with the peppers, gently mixing to combine.

Thinly slice the steak against the grain and divide among four plates. Top with the peppers and mushrooms and finish with another squeeze of lemon juice, if desired. Sprinkle generously with flaky salt.

THINGS WORTH SPENDING MONEY ON:

- BUTTER
- THERAPY
- MEAT
- MUSHROOMS
- TOMATOES
- FANCY SALT

THINGS NOT WORTH SPENDING MONEY ON:

- CLOTHES
- FRYING OIL
- A GARLIC PRESS
- NON STICK SAUTÉ PANS
- ICE CREAM SANDWICHES

DAWN

Homey Braised Beef Short Rib

Serves 4 • Prep time: 25 minutes • Cook time: 3 hours 35 minutes

- 2½ pounds boneless or 3½ pounds bone-in beef short ribs
- Kosher salt and freshly ground black pepper
- 2 tablespoons neutral oil
- 1 medium yellow onion (8 ounces), roughly chopped
- 2 medium carrots, peeled and roughly chopped
- 1 large celery stalk, roughly chopped
- 1 cup quartered trimmed button mushrooms (3 ounces)
- 3 garlic cloves, peeled but whole
- 2 cups red wine
- 1 tablespoon tomato paste
- 5 sprigs thyme
- 1 bay leaf
- 2 cups chicken stock or beef stock (see Note)
- 1 tablespoon cornstarch
- ¼ cup chopped parsley, for garnish
- Basic Spaetzle (page 186), for serving

Note: The chicken stock or beef stock will add flavor, but the beef is rich enough as it is, so if you're trying to keep costs down, feel free to replace with water.

Winter is depressing. Wake in darkness, sleep in darkness, dwell in darkness. But there's little in the world more comforting than a braised beef short rib on a wintry day. A lot of recipes for short rib overdo the red-wine reduction, which leads to a braised beef short rib that, basically, just tastes like red wine reduction and nothing else. Bummer. In this recipe, which I've always credited to Marco Canora, the well-respected chef of Hearth, the result is a cleaner and more versatile short rib that tastes like . . . short rib! (The Baxtrom touch is the mushrooms.) It's delicious the first day, the second day, and, atop Rehab Nachos (page 88), the third.

Preheat the oven to 300°F.

Season the short ribs generously with salt and pepper. In a large heavy-bottomed ovenproof pot, heat the oil over medium-high heat until shimmering. Working in two batches, add the short ribs and sear, flipping occasionally, until a golden brown and crispy crust forms on all sides, about 12 minutes total. Transfer the short ribs to a plate and set aside.

Meanwhile, in a food processor, pulse the onion, carrots, celery, mushrooms, and garlic until they form a coarse pulp.

Drain off the excess fat from the pot used for searing the meat. Add the red wine to the pot and bring to a boil over medium-high heat, stirring to pick up the browned bits from the bottom of the pot. Cook until the wine reduces by half and the alcohol evaporates, 10 to 12 minutes.

Stir in the processed vegetables and tomato paste and bring to a simmer. Return the seared short ribs to the pot. Place the thyme and bay leaf in a small sachet and add to the pot. Add the chicken stock, then add enough water to fully submerge the meat (about 4 cups). Season again with salt and pepper. Bring to a boil and transfer to the oven.

Cook for 3 hours, flipping the ribs halfway through the cooking time. The ribs are done when the internal temperature reaches around 200°F or the meat is falling off the bone.

Remove the ribs from the oven. In a small bowl, combine the cornstarch and 1 tablespoon water to create a slurry. Add the slurry to the liquid in the pot and place over medium-high heat. Bring to a boil until thickened to a gravy-like consistency. If desired, strain the sauce before serving for a smoother texture. Remove and discard the sachet.

Serve with the parsley and a side of Seasonal Affective Disorder or, better, spaetzle.

How to Make a Sachet

When I was growing up, a "sachet" was that little mesh bag my mom kept in the bathroom filled with potpourri. In the kitchen, it's actually the same idea: Chefs fill their sachets with fresh herbs and spices.

You can get little sachet bags from most restaurant supply stores or you can make one with cheesecloth: Just place the herbs in the center of a square of cheesecloth, then wrap it up and tie it closed with kitchen twine.

A Better Buttered Burger

Makes 4 burgers • Prep time: 20 minutes • Cook time: 10 minutes

Patti Ann's Secret Sauce

¼ medium red onion
½ jalapeño, seeded
¼ cup cornichons or chopped pickles
¼ cup canned fire-roasted tomatoes (or just ketchup, I guess)
2 canned chipotle peppers in adobo sauce
1 cup mayonnaise
1 teaspoon kosher salt
½ teaspoon smoked paprika

Burger Patties

8 tablespoons (4 ounces/1 stick) unsalted butter, frozen
1½ pounds ground brisket
Kosher salt and freshly ground black pepper

Assembly

2 tablespoons unsalted butter
4 potato buns, split
1 cup store-bought canned fried onions
8 slices sharp Cheddar cheese
Sliced tomatoes, for serving

Sherry Cardoso was the culinary director who oversaw the culinary staff, quality control, and morale for all my restaurants for years and she's put a craveable burger on the menu of every restaurant I own. (You try running a restaurant in New York City without a burger on the menu.) This one, from Patti Ann's, is one of my favorites. It's decadent and hits all the nostalgia notes you want from a burger, but with some flourish. It also caters to all short order cooks' love of smashing. They're not known for being patient people, and pressing something down on the flattop hastens the cooking.

This burger is made for them (and for any other impatient cooks), as everything—the burger and the bun—is smashed. The sear on the meat is super important for flavor and texture, the fried onions offer a perfect crunch, and our secret sauce—because every burger needs a secret sauce—is basically all the condiments and garnishes you want on a burger made into a spreadable sauce. But the hero of this recipe is the butter. So much butter, frozen and folded into the patties, acts as a self-baster, yielding rich and juicy patties.

Preheat the oven to 350°F.

Make Patti Ann's secret sauce: In a food processor, pulse together the onion, jalapeño, and cornichons until finely chopped. Add the fire-roasted tomatoes and chipotle peppers and pulse again a few times to chop. Add the mayonnaise, salt, and smoked paprika, pulsing a final time to combine. (The relish should have, well, a relish-y consistency.) Set aside.

Make the burger patties: Grate the frozen butter on the large holes of a box grater. In a stand mixer fitted with the paddle, mix together the beef and butter until uniform. Try not to overmix the meat.

Divide evenly into 4 patties about 5 inches in diameter and ½ inch thick. Season with salt and pepper.

To assemble: Heat a grill pan, a skillet, or a grill on medium-high. Melt the butter (you can do this in a small saucepan or in the microwave if working on a grill) and toast each split-side of the buns, pressing down hard with a spatula, about 1 minute. Remove the buns and set aside.

Increase the heat to high. Add the burger patties and cook until well charred, about 2 minutes on each side. Remove to a sheet pan. Divide the fried onions among the patties and top each with 2 slices of Cheddar. Place in the oven for 2 to 3 minutes to melt the cheese.

Fight your instincts with the bun, placing the outside face up (so the buttered inside faces outward). Apply as much secret sauce as you like in an even layer on the bottom bun. (I use about ¼ cup per burger.) Place the burger on the bun, top with sliced tomatoes, and add the top bun.

Hamburger Helper

Serves 4 • Prep time: 20 minutes • Cook time: 30 minutes

3 tablespoons neutral oil
1 pound 80/20 ground beef
1 yellow onion, thinly sliced
3 garlic cloves, minced
Kosher salt
3 cups elbow macaroni
3 cups beef broth or beef stock
One 15-ounce can tomato sauce
¾ cup heavy cream
1 tablespoon smoked paprika
1 tablespoon chili powder
1 tablespoon onion powder
1 tablespoon garlic powder
1 tablespoon dried oregano
1 teaspoon freshly ground black pepper
1 tablespoon Heirloom Pepper Hot Sauce (page 25)
8 ounces mild Cheddar cheese, shredded (2 cups)

My family was very active while I was growing up, so quick and easy meals were the name of the game. It fell to the first one home to get dinner going. Since we all ran cross-country and my parents didn't get home until 6 p.m., we kids were often the ones tasked with at least getting the meal started. A lot of my personal culinary practice was shaped by these recipes: pasta with tomato sauce, Salisbury steak with peas and noodles, and most of all, Hamburger Helper. By the time I was in high school and knew I wanted to be a chef, I'd make sure the dinner table was set and a candle was lit every night. (That was, I thought, part of what it meant to be a chef.) As my recipes grew from standard boxed things to slightly cheffier versions of them, I've never lost my taste for the satisfying part mac and cheese, part chili hybrid Hamburger Helper. The umami you grow up with is the umami you love.

In a large Dutch oven, heat the oil over medium-high heat until shimmering. Add the ground beef and cook, breaking up the meat with a spoon, until the fat is rendered, about 8 minutes.

Add the onion and garlic and season with salt. Reduce the heat to medium and cook, stirring frequently, until the beef is cooked through and browned and the onion is softened, 10 to 12 minutes.

Meanwhile, bring a large pot of salted water to a boil. Add the macaroni and cook according to the package directions. Drain and set aside.

Once the beef is cooked through, add the beef broth, tomato sauce, heavy cream, smoked paprika, chili powder, onion powder, garlic powder, oregano, pepper, and hot sauce, and season with salt. Bring to a simmer over medium heat and simmer for 5 minutes. Reduce the heat to low and gradually stir in the Cheddar until fully melted and creamy. Fold in the cooked pasta and adjust seasoning.

To serve, scoop and eat. No garnishes. No sides.

Cheese and Peppers Meatloaf

Serves 4 • Prep time: 25 minutes • Cook time: 1 hour

- 6 tablespoons extra-virgin olive oil
- ½ Spanish yellow onion, diced
- 3 garlic cloves, minced
- 1 roasted bell pepper (see Notes), diced
- 1 pound 80/20 ground beef
- 1 ounce cream cheese
- 1 cup diced Monterey Jack cheese
- 2 large eggs
- ¼ cup panko or Italian bread crumbs
- ½ cup Tomato Red Onion Ketchup (page 28; also see Notes)

There are many delicious things you can make with cheese, peppers, and ground beef. In fact, it would be hard to find a way to combine them that isn't going to be good. This meatloaf, basically a gargantuan cheeseburger, makes for a gooey, moist, and satisfying meal. As far as cheeses go, yeah, you could use ricotta (or even make your own, see page 72), but I typically use whatever cream cheese I have lying around to help keep the meat moist and make it smooth while the other cheese, Monterey Jack, is for flavor.

Preheat the oven to 350°F.

In a large sauté pan, heat 2 tablespoons of the olive oil over medium heat until shimmering. Add the onion and sauté until soft, about 6 minutes.

Add the garlic, allowing it to soften and turn lightly golden. Finally add the roasted pepper, stirring until incorporated. Remove from the heat and let cool.

In a stand mixer fitted with the paddle (or in a bowl by hand), combine the sautéed vegetables, beef, cream cheese, Monterey Jack, eggs, and panko and mix well.

Grease a 9-inch round pan, sauté pan, or anything that's ovenproof, really, with 2 tablespoons of olive oil and pack the meat in. Brush the meat with the remaining 2 tablespoons of olive oil and transfer to the oven.

Bake for 30 minutes. Remove and spread the ketchup evenly over the meatloaf and return to the oven for an additional 15 minutes.

Remove from the oven, let cool slightly, and serve.

Notes

- I like Dantza Red Sweet Piquillo Peppers, as they are beautifully roasted, peeled, and plump. They're consistently shaped, which makes them great for stuffing, too.
- I would add some smoked paprika to the ketchup if you have some lying around. Or, try swapping out the ketchup for Tonkatsu Sauce (page 96).

Lamb Shoulder Steak with One-Pot Couscous

Serves 4 • Prep time: 15 minutes • Cook time: 40 minutes

- Four 2-ounce Sweet Bunch carrots (see Guide below), tops trimmed, peeled, and cut on the bias into 1-inch obliques
- 2 tablespoons unsalted butter
- ½ teaspoon sugar
- Kosher salt and freshly ground black pepper
- 1 cup shelled English peas
- 1 cup fine couscous
- ¼ cup loosely packed fresh parsley leaves, coarsely chopped
- 4 bone-in lamb shoulder steaks (6 ounces each), ½ inch thick
- Extra-virgin olive oil, for rubbing
- 1 Garlic Fork (see page 53)

Lamb shoulder is a more forgiving steak. It's less intimidating than a rack of lamb and less of a hassle than lamb T-bones. The lamb shoulder is only about ½ inch thick, which makes it easier to obtain that perfect medium-rare and tender cook you're looking for. (Lamb gets chewy when overcooked.) From a flavor standpoint, it's not overwhelmingly lamby because there's not too much fat. Couscous is a classic pairing for lamb, and this one is incredibly easy to make. It's filled with springtime vegetables and made with a simplified beurre monté (an emulsified butter sauce), which yields glossy flavorful carrots, peas with a bit of a pop, and fluffy grains.

Preheat the oven to 350°F.

In a medium sauté pan, combine the carrots and just enough water to cover them. Add the butter and sugar and season with a big pinch of salt and a few cracks of pepper. Heat over medium-high heat until simmering, then allow to cook until the water is gone and the carrots are fork tender, 18 to 20 minutes.

Add 1 cup water and the peas. Return to a boil, then add the couscous and season again with salt and pepper. Cover, reduce the heat to low, and simmer for 15 minutes. Once the couscous is puffy, fluff it up with a fork and stir in the parsley and season to taste. Set aside, covering to keep warm.

Meanwhile, heat a large grill pan over high heat. Rub the lamb lightly with olive oil and season generously with salt and pepper. Once the pan is hot, add the lamb and cook until you get some nice grill marks on both sides, about 2 minutes per side. Transfer to the oven and cook until medium-rare, 2 to 3 minutes, depending on the thickness of the steak. Remove and transfer the steaks to a cutting board to rest for a few minutes. While the lamb rests, use a trusty garlic fork to rub garlic on the meat.

Slice the lamb and serve over the vegetables and couscous.

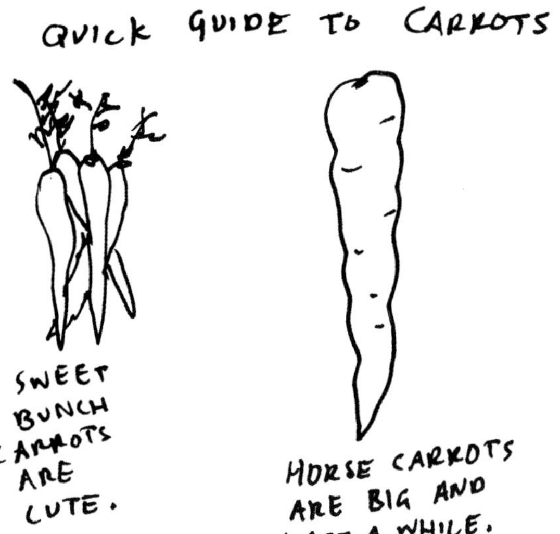

~~Curried Lamb and Pork Sausage~~
~~Curried Pork Sausage~~
~~Curried Lamb Sausage~~
Whatever. Sausage.

Makes 2 pounds 4 ounces • Prep time: 20 minutes • Cook time: n/a • Inactive time: 30 minutes to 1 hour

- 1 pound lamb leg, cut into 1-inch pieces
- 1 pound pork shoulder, cut into 1-inch pieces
- One 1-inch thumb fresh ginger, peeled and roughly chopped
- 2 garlic cloves, peeled but whole
- 1 bunch fresh cilantro
- 1 Fresno chile, stemmed and seeded
- 1 teaspoon pink curing salt
- 2 teaspoons kosher salt
- 2 teaspoons sugar
- ¼ cup curry powder

Making homemade sausage sounds like an activity for mustachioed artisans with lots of tattoos and a deep commitment to the handmade. It's not; anyone can do it. Well, anyone with a meat grinder. By far the most onerous part of making sausage is the casing, and the good news is: Who cares about casing? (One of the purposes of the casing is that it holds in the juices, but even without casing, there's plenty of juice to go around.) And liberated from a casing, there's so much you can do with the sausage filling: patties, meatballs, terrine, you name it.

For me, what makes sausage so satisfying is the ratio of fat to lean meat. Get that right and each bite explodes with flavor. This recipe is more improvisatory than rote. By using a 1:1 ratio of pork shoulder and lamb leg—though you can tweak these to your taste by, for instance, zealously guarding the pork shoulder but swapping out those duck legs from the Duck Confit (page 79) or maybe those chicken thighs from the chicken crowns you made (see page 129) for the lamb—you are naturally getting pretty close to the fat to lean ratio you'll need. The curry powder, ginger, and cilantro add a sausage-y symphony of flavor. The pink curing salt, meanwhile, acts both as a flavoring agent and a method of preservation.

In a stand mixer fitted with the paddle attachment, combine the lamb, pork shoulder, ginger, garlic, cilantro, chile, pink curing salt, kosher salt, sugar, and curry powder. Mix until combined and place in the freezer for 30 minutes to 1 hour, until firmed up a bit.

Using a meat grinder attachment, grind the meat mixture through the small die plate right back into the mixer bowl. Add ¼ cup cold water and mix with the paddle on low speed until tacky, about 1 minute.

Now you have your embryonic sausage. You can do a couple of things with it (ideas follow).

SAUSAGE PATTIES

Makes about 16 patties

Whatever. Sausage. (page 150)

1 tablespoon extra-virgin olive oil

Preheat the oven to 350°F.

Divide the meat into 16 equal portions (about ¼ cup each) and form into patties about ¼ inch thick.

Heat an ovenproof sauté pan over medium heat. Add the olive oil and heat until shimmering. Cooking in batches if needed, add the patties and sear on one side for about 2 minutes, or until well browned. Flip the patties and transfer to the oven.

Bake until cooked through, about 3 minutes.

Sausage patties can be stored 3 days in the refrigerator or frozen up to 1 month.

LAYERLESS TERRINE

This goes great in sandwiches like banh mi, as a side to fried eggs, or you can dice it and add it to ragù, a pasta, or a soup. Because it's a bouncy little sausage log, you should treat it like it's ham, not sausage, and add to recipes accordingly.

Makes one 10-by-10-inch or two 5-by-5-inch terrines

Whatever. Sausage. (page 150)

Note: The brick has to fit into a wide shallow pan. If you don't have one big enough, divide the meat into two 1-quart bags and then cook in batches.

Place the sausage mixture into a 1 gallon zip-seal plastic bag (see Note), compressing it as much as possible into a flat, even brick-like shape, about ¾ inch thick. Press out as much air as possible and seal the bag well, with tape.

Fill a sauté or other wide shallow pan (large enough to fit the brick) halfway up with water and bring to a simmer over medium heat. Once simmering, add the sausage in the bag and cook for 10 minutes on one side. Flip and cook for an additional 10 minutes.

Remove and let cool completely in the bag before using.

Layerless terrine can be stored 3 days in the refrigerator or frozen up to 1 month.

SAUSAGE MEATBALLS

Makes 36 meatballs

Whatever. Sausage. (page 150)

Extra-virgin olive oil

Preheat the oven to 350°F.

Put the sausage filling in the refrigerator for 30 minutes until cool. (This makes rolling them easier.)

Remove from the fridge and roll the meat into 2-tablespoon (1-ounce) balls about 1½ inches in diameter. Place them on a sheet pan and drizzle the tops lightly with some olive oil.

Bake until cooked through, 10 to 12 minutes.

Meatballs can be stored 3 days in the refrigerator or frozen up to 1 month.

Some Kinda Larb

Serves 4 • Prep time: 15 minutes • Cook time: 15 minutes

2 tablespoons neutral oil
1 pound ground meat (turkey, duck, beef, chicken, or pork)
½ medium red onion, thinly sliced
Thai Dressing (page 111)
3 tablespoons cornstarch
¼ cup fresh shiso leaves
¼ cup fresh mint leaves
¼ cup fresh basil leaves
¼ cup Thai Crunchy Topping (page 111)
1 cucumber (8 ounces), thinly sliced
1 head Bibb lettuce (or whatever other soft buttery lettuce), washed and dried

Restaurant chefs exist on takeout. Who wants to cook after a long shift in the kitchen? Not me. All I want to do is collapse into my sofa and watch *Three's Company* until I pass out. Thankfully, my neighborhood in Brooklyn is full of amazing restaurants like Look by Plant Love House, a Thai restaurant opened by Manadsanan Sutipayakul and her daughters. While their spot has since closed (I was heartbroken), while it was around the corner from my apartment I survived on their spicy watercress salad, poke mau, papaya salad, and above all, their larb, a spicy Laotian minced meat salad. You can still technically order their old menu from their new spot, Noods n' Chill, in Williamsburg, but that's beyond my delivery zone, so I made this as an homage. Make it if you want. Most of the ingredients—fish sauce, palm sugar, a lime leaf that lives in your freezer—are evergreen, but if you can, order it from them—their version is much better.

In a large sauté pan, heat the oil over high heat until shimmering. Add the ground meat, using a spatula to break it up, and cook, stirring once or twice, until mostly cooked through, 4 to 5 minutes.

Add the red onion and sauté until the meat is cooked and browned in places and the onion has softened but not completely cooked through, 4 to 5 minutes.

Reduce the heat to medium-low and add the Thai Dressing. Continue to cook for 1 to 2 more minutes to allow the dressing to commingle with the meat.

Meanwhile, in a small bowl, combine the cornstarch and 3 tablespoons room temperature water and whisk together to form a slurry.

Add the cornstarch slurry to the pan. As soon as it returns to a low simmer, remove from the heat.

Serve the dish with the shiso leaves, mint leaves, basil leaves, Thai Crunchy Topping, cucumber, and lettuce.

One-Pan Pork Chop with Everyone in the Pool Sauce

Serves 4 • Prep time: 20 minutes • Cook time: 40 minutes

Kosher salt
1 pound small new potatoes (see Note), halved
4 bone-in pork chops (about 11 ounces each), 1 inch thick (see below)
Freshly ground black pepper
¾ cup plus 2 tablespoons all-purpose flour
2 tablespoons neutral oil, plus more as needed
½ head cauliflower (about 1 pound), cut into 2-inch florets
8 ounces cremini mushrooms, stemmed and thickly sliced
3 garlic cloves, grated
1 bunch green onions (6 or 7), thinly sliced, white and dark green parts separated
1 plum tomato (7 ounces), cored and diced
2 tablespoons unsalted butter
¼ cup heavy cream

Note: New potatoes are the Ferraris of potatoes. These spring vegetables are incredibly buttery and naturally flavorful, so you hardly have to do anything to them.

I am told people like sauce. I am also aware that they are intimidated by making it. I understand the former but not the latter. Preparing a delicious pan sauce can be simple. You are basically using the *fond*—the flavorful leftover solids you have from roasting a protein—as a base for a gravy. Simple, right?

When you're making a sauce, you need to do a few things: First, get the bits off the pan and into the mix. That's called deglazing, which I do here by using the liquid the mushrooms release into the pan to loosen the bits. Second, you add flavor—i.e., a bunch o' vegetables. Note here that these veggies must be prepped before they go in and also that their released liquid helps build the sauce. That's it. Everyone gets in the pool. Once you have the flavor, build a body, which I do here with a roux (a fancy word for butter and flour mixed together and melted), cream, and starchy potato water. There you go. Pretty easy. Really good.

Preheat the oven to 350°F.

Bring a large pot of salted water to a boil.

Add the potatoes to the boiling water and cook until fork-tender, 10 to 12 minutes. Reserving 1 cup of the starchy potato liquid, drain the potatoes.

Season the pork with salt and pepper. Add ¾ cup of the flour to a plate and dredge each chop. Shake off to remove excess flour.

In a large cast-iron skillet, heat the oil over medium-high heat until it shimmers. Working in batches to avoid crowding the pan, add the pork chops and sear until golden brown on both sides, 3 to 4 minutes per side. Set the pork chops on a sheet pan and transfer to the oven. Reserve the skillet.

Bake until cooked through (the chops should register about 145°F on a meat thermometer), 6 to 8 minutes.

Let the chops rest for 10 minutes, then cut into ¼-inch slices.

Rinse the cauliflower florets in cold water and place uncovered in a microwave-safe bowl. Microwave for 3 to 4 minutes until steamed and just tender.

Return the skillet in which you cooked the pork to medium-high heat, adding more oil if needed for cooking the mushrooms. Once shimmering, add the mushrooms and cook, stirring once or twice, until golden brown, about 4 minutes. Add the steamed cauliflower and garlic, stirring well to combine. Add the whites of the green onions, the potatoes, and tomato, stirring well. Once everything is well combined, add the butter and remaining 2 tablespoons of flour. Cook until the butter melts and the flour is incorporated to form a roux, about 2 minutes. Stir in the cream and the 1 cup reserved potato water, stirring until combined and thickened just a bit, another minute or two. Check seasoning for a final time.

To serve, spoon the sauce and potatoes on the bottom of a plate, then layer on sliced pork, bone, and finish with greens of the the sliced green onions.

THIS WHOLE RECIPE, BTW, WORKS WITH ANY SORT OF PROTEIN. IT DOESN'T HAVE TO BE PORK CHOPS. AND YOU KNOW WHAT? THE VEGETABLES DON'T REALLY MATTER ANYWAY. NOTHING MATTERS! YOU CAN USE EGGPLANT, KOHLRABI, BELL PEPPERS, GREEN BEANS OR SWEET POTATOES. YOU GET THE IDEA. THROW THEM ALL IN THE POOL AND LET'S GO!

Super-Crunch Pork Nugs with Blood Orange Sweet and Sour Sauce

Serves 4 • Prep time: 20 minutes • Cook time: 20 minutes

1 cup egg whites (8 to 10 large eggs)
¾ cup cornstarch
1 pound ground pork
2 tablespoons Baxtrom Spice (page 19)
2 cups panko bread crumbs
Canola oil
Kosher salt
For serving: Blood Orange Sweet and Sour Sauce (page 29), Tomato Red Onion Ketchup (page 28), Heirloom Pepper Hot Sauce (page 25), or really anything

Using a cornstarch and egg white mixture for breading, instead of the traditional flour, egg whites, and bread crumbs, is a Thomas Keller technique I learned at Per Se. It yields super-crispy nuggets that are crispy even when you put them in the fridge and reheat them the next day. While the breading begins at Per Se, the rest of this recipe is pure McDonald's nostalgia. Nuggets, as every kid knows, mostly function as delicious vehicles for sauce. The first time I made these was as a way to get more sweet and sour sauce into my mouth, but the nuggets themselves were so juicy and crunchy, soon I was using them as a highway for mayo, mustard, ketchup, hot sauce, whatever I could find. You'll end up doing the same.

In a large bowl, whisk together the egg whites and cornstarch until well incorporated.

Form the ground pork into 16 meatballs (1 ounce each) and then gently flatten them to become more nuggety. (Or not, and this turns into Super-Crunch Pork *Meatballs.*) Season with the Baxtrom Spice.

Add the pork nuggets to the cornstarch slurry and gently toss until well coated.

Spread the panko bread crumbs on a sheet pan or a plate.

Set a wire rack in a sheet pan and have near the stove. Pour about 1 inch oil (see Note) into a large heavy-bottomed pot and heat over medium heat until shimmering.

Working in batches, remove the nuggets from the slurry, letting the excess drip back into the bowl. Coat each piece in the panko, pressing to adhere, and then add them to the oil, making sure not to crowd the pan. Fry until golden brown, 4 to 5 minutes per side. Transfer to the wire rack to drain. Season immediately with salt.

Serve with Blood Orange Sweet and Sour Sauce, Tomato Red Onion Ketchup, Heirloom Pepper Hot Sauce, or any sauce of choice.

Note: You can deep-fry or shallow-fry these nuggets, it doesn't make a difference. In my house, I shallow-fry so I don't have a bunch of extra oil to deal with. If I am shallow-frying, I use a larger-than-normal pan with high sides to catch the splatter.

Roast Pork with Noods

Serves 4 • Prep time: 25 minutes • Cook time: 1 hour

- 1½-pound piece boneless pork shoulder
- Kosher salt and freshly ground black pepper
- 3 tablespoons any spice rub
- 2 tablespoons neutral oil, plus more as needed
- 1 pound lo mein or alkaline noodles
- 1 red bell pepper (6 ounces), diced (1 cup)
- 1 head broccoli (12 ounces), all of it, diced (3 cups)
- 1 medium red onion (8 ounces), diced (1½ cups)
- ¼ cup oyster sauce
- 1 Ginger Purse (recipe follows)
- 1 cup fresh cilantro or basil leaves
- 1 tablespoon toasted black and white sesame seeds

To not use oyster sauce and premade spice rubs is to deprive oneself of the labor of others. And for what? Pride? Egotism? A weird fixation on the homemade? Why is it, for instance, that a chef is applauded when he lets nature do the work by bringing forth products—Watermelon! Fluke! Kale!—intervening only minimally, but when that same chef, for instance, dips into his pantry to use a well-considered premade spice rub or ajvar or kimchi or umami-rich deeply flavored oyster sauce, he is impugned as a wastrel? Maybe he isn't. Maybe this is just the internal monologue of a deeply conflicted chef who was raised to grind, coming to terms with the ease and rulelessness of home cooking, as he makes a succulent pork noodle dish bursting with flavor having done virtually no work at all.

Preheat the oven to 350°F.

Lightly season the pork with salt, pepper, and your spice rub of choice.

In a large sauté pan, heat the oil over medium-high heat until shimmering. Add the pork and sear evenly on all sides until golden brown, about 2 minutes per side. Remove the pork from the pan, set on a sheet pan, and transfer to the oven. Set the sauté pan aside.

Roast the pork until the internal temperature reaches 145°F, 40 to 45 minutes. Transfer to a cutting board and let rest for at least 10 minutes.

Meanwhile, bring a large pot of salted water to a boil. Add the noodles and cook according to the package directions. Drain, rinse, and set aside.

Rinse the bell pepper, broccoli, and onion in cold water, drain well, then transfer to a large bowl. Cover with a microwave-safe plate and microwave for 2 to 4 minutes, until tender. Drain again and set aside.

If there are any burnt bits at the bottom of the reserved sauté pan, wipe them away with a paper towel. Place the pan over medium heat, adding more oil if needed. Once shimmering, add the steamed vegetables to the pan, stirring well to combine. Add the oyster sauce and squeeze out the ginger juice from your purse—you should get about ¼ cup—and stir to combine. Add the noodles and give everything one more toss.

Slice the roast pork into ¼-inch-thick slices. Serve the noodles in a bowl and top with the sliced pork. Add the cilantro and finish with a mix of black and white sesame seeds.

Making a Ginger Purse

Basically a ginger purse is a way to get a burst of ginger flavor without having to mince or grate ginger, which is the worst. Because what happens is you take a knob of ginger and all the weird pieces that are too hard to get your peeler into and you end up peeling something the size of an eraser and you're cutting the heck out of your fingers.

So do this instead: Take those pieces, about a cup of them, and just wash them (no peeling) and then blitz them in a food processor for like 10 seconds. Take that mush and wrap it in cheesecloth—or even a folded-up paper towel, doesn't matter—and tie it in a pretty little purse. Then you just squeeze it to get ginger juice.

It's best to use it fresh, but it'll last a week in a Tupperware container. Whenever you want a burst of ginger, squeeze it in.

Prosciutto-Wrapped Pork Tenderloin

Serves 4 • Prep time: 25 minutes • Cook time: 45 minutes • Inactive time: 1 hour

- 2 pork tenderloins
- Kosher salt and freshly ground black pepper
- 20 slices prosciutto
- 1 bunch fresh sage, leaves picked and finely chopped
- 2 tablespoons extra-virgin olive oil
- 1 cup Brussels sprouts, trimmed and halved
- ½ bunch Sweet Bunch carrots, peeled and cut in half lengthwise (see page 149)

Note: Don't know what the silverskin is? It's the thin, tough, silvery membrane you'll find around tenderloins. (Pork, beef, lamb, rabbit . . . really any tenderloin.) It's not edible and can fuck up the meat by constricting it as it cooks so the meat gets distorted and hunched over. It's best to remove it. Make an incision with a sharp knife, then, working the knife between the meat and silverskin, work your way down the tenderloin.

Before he became a world-famous competitive eater, Pat "Deep Dish" Bertoletti—who has eaten 13 pounds of tartine in 10 minutes and drunk 2½ gallons of milk in an hour—was my roommate at culinary school. At the time, we were just nineteen-year-old kids with little kitchen experience, but Pat had somehow raffled off a dinner that he would cook for a family of twelve through his church. He asked me to help. It was the first time we wrote a menu: grilled calamari to start, and a prosciutto-wrapped herb-crusted pork tenderloin as the main course. My girlfriend at the time proposed orange soufflés inside the oranges themselves as dessert. Nearly everything was a disaster. We had to set up a grill outside in the middle of winter for the calamari, which left our fingertips simultaneously frozen and burnt. We baked the soufflés for 30 minutes before realizing the oven wasn't on. The only bright spot was the tenderloin, a recipe I came up with inspired by a Jamie Oliver recipe. I still make it to this day, especially when I visit my parents for the holidays. It's perfect for them because it's just on that borderline between normal and cheffy—my parents love it because it feels like normal holiday food and it's easy enough that I don't hate making it.

Clean the silverskin (see Note) off the pork with a sharp knife. Pat the tenderloins dry, then season well with salt and pepper.

On a work surface, shingle enough of the prosciutto, overlapping each slice by half, until you've achieved the length of one of the tenderloins. Place the tenderloin on one edge of the prosciutto carpet and roll it up like a body. Repeat with the second tenderloin and remaining prosciutto.

Spread the sage on the cutting board and season with black pepper. Roll the pork in the sage until evenly coated. Wrap the tenderloins tightly in plastic wrap and leave in the fridge for at least 1 hour. (The longer it sits, the better.)

When ready to cook, remove the tenderloins from the refrigerator and let come to room temperature.

Preheat the oven to 350°F.

Heat a large ovenproof sauté pan over high heat and add the olive oil. Once shimmering, add one of the tenderloins, searing on all sides, about 6 minutes total, about 2 minutes a side. Remove and repeat with the second tenderloin.

Add the Brussels sprouts cut-side down to the pan, then add the carrots. Cook until the edges start to show some color, about 6 minutes for the Brussels sprouts, 20 minutes for the carrots. Set the pork atop the vegetables and transfer to the oven.

Cook until the pork reaches an internal temperature of 145°F, about 15 minutes.

To serve, let the pork rest for 10 minutes or so. Slice into ½-inch-thick slices and serve with the vegetables on the side.

A Sausage and Some Greens

Serves 4 • Prep time: 25 minutes • Cook time: 25 minutes

2 tablespoons extra-virgin olive oil
4 links of your favorite specialty sausage (or Whatever. Sausage., page 150, sliced into small pieces)
2 tablespoons unsalted butter
1 pound button mushrooms, stemmed and thinly sliced
Kosher salt and freshly ground black pepper
1 Garlic Fork (see page 53)
8 cups baby greens
½ lemon

Sometimes you just see a sausage in a case at your butcher shop and it calls to you—you want to take it home and get to know it and invite it to a sausage party. The flavor combinations are endless and mouthwatering: bacon and jalapeño, truffle and duck, cheese-filled andouille bratwurst. If you buy yourself a nice specialty sausage, you need to treat it right—it should be the star of the show, it should feel special. A great sausage doesn't need a complicated side dish, and these unfussy greens are the perfect accompaniment. Cooked perfectly, they should be undersautéed—just in the waiting room of sautéed but not quite there. You want a little crunch, a little texture, and they shouldn't be too wet to detract from the snap of the sausage.

Preheat the oven to 350°F.

In an ovenproof sauté pan, heat 1 tablespoon of the olive oil over high heat until shimmering. Add the sausage and sauté for 2 minutes, flip over and sauté another 2 minutes, then pop in the oven for 6 minutes till fully cooked through.

Meanwhile, in a separate sauté pan, heat the remaining 1 tablespoon of olive oil and the butter over medium-high heat until the oil shimmers and the butter is melted. Add the mushrooms, season with salt and pepper, and stir with the garlic fork. Sauté the mushrooms until they soften and begin to brown, 4 to 5 minutes.

Add the baby greens and continue to sauté, stirring with the garlic fork, until the greens are half wilted and half cooked through, 1 to 2 minutes. Remove from the heat and squeeze the lemon over top. Check for seasoning a final time.

Remove the sausage from the oven if you haven't already and let it rest for 5 minutes. Then slice into ¼-inch coins and serve atop the greens.

BUT WHAT IF MY SAUSAGE ISN'T DONE? YEAH, SOMETIMES YOU PULL IT OUT TOO EARLY AND WHEN YOU CUT INTO THE SAUSAGE, IT'S STILL PINK IN THE CENTER. WHO CARES? STOP CUTTING IT. SMOOSH THE TWO PIECES BACK TOGETHER, RETURN THEM TO THE OVEN FOR ANOTHER COUPLE OF MINUTES, AND THEN START THE RESTING PROCESS OVER AGAIN.

FISH

Cod Almondine

Serves 4 • Prep time: 20 minutes • Cook time: 20 minutes

- 4 skinless cod fillets (6 ounces each), about 1 inch thick
- Kosher salt and freshly ground black pepper
- 2 tablespoons neutral oil
- 4 tablespoons unsalted butter, cubed
- 2 handfuls green beans, trimmed
- ½ red onion, thinly sliced
- 3 garlic cloves, minced
- 1 handful slivered almonds, crushed in your clenched fist in existential rage
- 1 large tomato, cored and diced
- 1 lemon, halved

Amandine, or almondine as it is Americanized, is a classic French preparation that uses butter and almonds. The most famous almondine dishes are trout almondine and green beans almondine, but you can use any sort of whitefish in place of the trout: cod, hake, sable. Obviously, the star of the show is the slivered and crushed almonds, but the key to the dish is the butter, which lets the ingredients glisten and shine. Let's just be honest: The key to 90 percent of classic French recipes is the butter. When making an almondine, you don't want to burn the almonds—bitter!—and you don't want to overcook the fish—dry! In this recipe, by allowing the fish to basically poach in the butter off the heat, you almost guarantee the fish will be perfectly cooked through without drying out.

Pat the fish fillets dry and then season both sides with salt and pepper.

In a sauté pan, heat the oil over medium-high heat until shimmering. Add the fillets one at a time, waiting 30 seconds after each one to allow the pan to recover. Sear until mostly cooked and beginning to flake, 2 to 3 minutes. Add the butter to the pan, and once it is melted, gently flip the fillets, remove from the heat, and allow to low-key poach in the butter* until fully cooked, about 4 minutes.

Rinse the green beans well, place in a microwave-safe bowl, and microwave for about 2 minutes, or until tender.

Remove the fillets from the pan using a fish spatula (if you have one) and set aside. Return the butter to medium heat. Once the butter begins to pop, add the onion and garlic. Cook, stirring occasionally, until translucent, 4 to 5 minutes.

Add the almonds and cook until fragrant and lightly toasted, about 4 minutes. Stir in the tomato, toss in the green beans, season with salt and pepper, and remove from the heat.

To serve, spread the vegetables on a platter and top with the fish. To finish, squeeze the lemon over the whole thing.

*This is a super lazy way to baste.

Clams à la Han Dynasty

Serves 2 • Prep time: 5 minutes • Cook time: 10 minutes

- 2 dozen littleneck clams (2½ pounds)
- 2 tablespoons soy sauce
- 1 tablespoon cornstarch
- 8 ounces asparagus, ends trimmed, cut into 1-inch pieces
- All the spicy goodness (¼ to ⅓ cup) left over from 1 order of dry pepper chicken from Han Dynasty (see Note)

Note: Look, you may not live near a Han Dynasty. Statistically you probably don't. But I guarantee that you live near a Chinese takeout place and that they most likely have some version of this chicken on the menu. Use that. And generally, if you have leftover sauce or whatever when you get takeout, don't throw it out. Experiment with how to leverage all that delicious flavor in another application.

Han Chiang and his mother, Lung Lung, opened Han Dynasty, my favorite Sichuan restaurant, in New York City in 2007. Since then, they've expanded into ten locations in Philly and New York. I order from the location in Brooklyn at least once a week. My go-to order is the dry pepper chicken and the pea shoots. The dry pepper chicken, also called *laziji* or Chongqing, after the region from which it comes, is made of chunks of fried chicken topped with an ungodly amount of dried chile peppers. The joke is the spicier you order it, the less chicken you get, so you want a good mix. I order it a lot and it kills me to let all those peppers go to waste. You know that saying "Waste not, want not"? In professional kitchens, it's waste not, waste not. Sometimes I'll just pour a neutral oil over the chiles and make a chile oil. But if I want something more substantial, I've found that the clam broth left over from steaming clams boasts a concentrated briny flavor that is irresistible in combination with the heat of the Sichuan peppers. It's two Han Dynasty dinners for the price of one.

Heat a large deep-sided pot over high heat until ripping hot. Add the clams and 1 cup water and immediately cover with a lid. Allow to cook until the clams have opened, 4 to 5 minutes.

Meanwhile, in a small bowl, whisk together the soy sauce, cornstarch, and 1 cup water until smooth.

Once the clams have opened, add the soy sauce mixture to the pot with the clams, then reduce the heat to medium and cook uncovered for about 2 minutes to thicken the sauce to the consistency of a loose gravy.

Meanwhile, place the asparagus in a microwave-safe bowl with a splash of water and cover with a microwave-safe plate. Microwave for about 2 minutes, or until tender, then drain off any liquid.

Add the asparagus and the spicy leftover goodness to the clams, discarding any that haven't opened, and toss to combine. Serve immediately.

Neo-Fjordic Oysters

Serves 4 • Prep time: 25 minutes • Cook time: 1 hour

Pickled Beets (recipe follows)
¼ cup Pickled Beets liquid
1 teaspoon preserved horseradish, finely chopped (Gold's preferred)
¼ cup crème fraîche
Kosher salt
Crushed ice
24 Island Creek oysters, shucked
1 lemon, halved
1 ounce smoked trout roe
24 small dill sprigs

"Neo-Fjordic" doesn't really mean anything at all. But when my best friend, Chris Haatuft of the fine-dining restaurant Lysverket in Bergen, Norway, was asked his style in an interview with the *New York Times*, he just made it up and it stuck. Now he's the godfather of Neo-Fjordic cuisine. Chris and I met at Alinea and worked together at Stone Barns. Even though we couldn't seem any more different (he's got a gold tooth, a flying bat with rather large testicles tattooed on his chest, and knows more about wine than most sommes in New York), we hit it off. He's hardworking, really funny, inventive as hell, and, most important, incredibly kind. When I was struggling with suicidal ideations, he flew to New York to help me, well, survive. When I opened Olmsted, I wanted to pay homage to my friend with these oysters, which are basically just a bunch of Scando ingredients thrown into an oyster, which happens to taste delicious.

Also, colored ice is a neat party trick. You literally have to do no work for a high reward.

Finely dice the beets and place them, along with the cooled pickling liquid, in the refrigerator.

In a small bowl, combine the horseradish and crème fraîche. Season with salt and whisk until soft peaks form.

To serve, place crushed ice in a large wide bowl. Toss the cooled beet pickling liquid with the ice to make it pink.

Place the oysters atop the ice and squeeze the lemon over them. Add a dime-size pile of the beets to each oyster, then a similar size dollop of the horseradish crème fraîche. Top each oyster with 1 teaspoon trout roe and a sprig of dill and serve.

PICKLED BEETS

Pickled beets stored in their pickling liquid in the fridge last for a very long time. You can use them to make a No-Big-Deal Roasted Beet Salad (page 53) or drain and blend a cup or two into the Spaetzle dough (see page 186) for romantic pink spaetzle.

Serves 4

1 bunch beets, trimmed and rinsed
2 tablespoons extra-virgin olive oil
Kosher salt and freshly ground black pepper
1 quart House Pickling Liquid (page 38)

Preheat the oven to 350°F.

Rub the beets well with the olive oil, season with salt and pepper, wrap loosely in foil, and roast until fork-tender, about 1 hour.

Meanwhile, in a saucepan, bring the pickling liquid to a boil.

When the beets are done, remove from the oven and, using gloves, peel the skin off while still hot. Add the beets to a large heatproof bowl and pour the boiling pickling liquid over top. Set aside and let cool completely before refrigerating. Pickled beets can keep in the refrigerator for one month.

Seared Salmon with Spring Pistou

Serves 4 • Prep time: 30 minutes • Cook time: 20 minutes

Pistou

2 cups broccoli florets and stems
¼ medium yellow onion, thinly sliced
1 celery stalk, thinly sliced
3 garlic cloves, peeled but whole
½ cup fresh basil leaves, plus sprigs for garnish
1 tablespoon unsalted butter
Kosher salt and freshly ground black pepper

Veggies

4 fingerling potatoes
Kosher salt
8 cherry tomatoes
4 baby carrots, peeled and halved lengthwise
1 Persian (mini) cucumber

To Finish

2 tablespoons extra-virgin olive oil, plus more as needed
4 skin-on salmon fillets (6 ounces each), about 1 inch thick
Kosher salt and freshly ground black pepper
Juice of ½ lemon (1 to 2 tablespoons)

You'll find pistou, an olive oil–based sauce, all over the South of France. It's a close cousin to the better-known Genovese pesto, a green sauce made with basil and garlic. (*Pistou* and *pesto* both really just mean "pounded" or "ground.") Usually pistou is served cold and thick, like a pesto, or else incorporated into a minestrone-like soup called soupe au pistou. But my version is itself a bit more soupy and served warm, poured tableside so it seems fancier than just a bunch of vegetables you blended. I like it because it's bright green and easygoing, like the Hulk on molly.

Though pistou is traditionally made with basil, Parmesan, and olive oil, here the main body of the sauce is broccoli, and instead of olive oil, I use butter for a rich silken sauce. File this under: sounds fancy, is a cinch.

Preheat the oven to 350°F.

Make the pistou: In a medium saucepan, bring 3 cups water to a boil over high heat. Once boiling, add the broccoli, onion, celery, and garlic and boil for 5 minutes.

Transfer the vegetables, their cooking water, the basil, and butter to a blender. Season with salt and pepper and blend until smooth. Check for seasoning. Cover to keep warm and set aside.

Prep the veggies: In a small saucepan, combine the potatoes with water to cover completely. Season generously with salt. Bring to a boil and cook until the potatoes are fork-tender, 8 to 10 minutes. Lift from the water (but keep the pan on the stove) and let cool slightly, then use a paring knife to gently peel away the skins.

Add the tomatoes to the boiling water and cook for 30 to 60 seconds, just until the skins begin to split. Lift from the water and peel.

Add the carrots to the boiling water and cook until tender, about 3 minutes. Drain.

Halve the cucumber lengthwise, then cut on a bias into ½-inch-thick slices.

To finish: In a large heavy-bottomed pan, heat the olive oil over medium heat until shimmering. Pat the salmon dry and season with salt and pepper. Add the fillets to the pan one at a time, skin-side down, waiting 30 seconds after each one to allow the pan to recover. Gently press against the fillets with a spatula to flatten if they begin to curl up. Once you see the edges starting to brown, 2 to 3 minutes, transfer the pan to the oven.

Bake until the skin is crisp and the fillets are cooked through, about 4 minutes. Remove the pan from the oven, flip the fillets, and let rest for a few minutes.

Toss the cucumber and tomato together with a splash of olive oil and season with salt.

Stir the lemon juice into the pistou.

Plate it fancy using four separate wide shallow bowls. First place a fillet in the bottom of the bowl, skin-side up, then divide the vegetables among the bowls. Add the pistou, tableside, pouring around each salmon fillet. Finish with some reserved basil sprigs.

FUCK, MY FISH STUCK TO THE PAN. FISH STICKS TO A PAN THAT ISN'T HOT ENOUGH. IF YOUR SALMON STICKS, IT'S NOT THE END OF THE WORLD. JUST REDUCE THE HEAT TO MEDIUM AND BE PATIENT. EVENTUALLY THE MOISTURE WILL COOK OUT OF THE SKIN AND THE FISH WILL RELEASE.

Summer Scallop Succotash

Serves 4 • Prep time: 20 minutes • Cook time: 25 minutes

1 pound scallops (about 18)
¼ cup Pasilla Chile Dry Rub (page 20)
Kosher salt
2 tablespoons neutral oil, plus more as needed
3 large ears corn (2¼ pounds total), kernels cut off the cob (about 2 cups)
12 ounces shiitake mushrooms, stemmed and quartered (1¾ cups)
2 fresh banana peppers (3 ounces total), thinly sliced
1½ cups Sungold tomatoes (9 ounces), halved
¾ cup shelled edamame
3 tablespoons unsalted butter
3 tablespoons sour cream
1½ tablespoons chopped fresh tarragon

This is a recipe about SUMMER, SCALLOPS, and SIZE.

Nothing summons SUMMER like an ear of sweet corn. Every vegetable in this recipe—the tomatoes, the mushrooms, the edamame, the peppers, whatever—is interchangeable, but the sweetness of the corn is not. If you don't have peak summer corn, do not make this succotash. (Technically, you can't anyway, since what makes a succotash a succotash *is* the corn.)

SCALLOPS can be tricky. Well-seared, they're slightly sweet, tender pleasure buttons. But overcooked, they're chewy and unpleasant and stick to the pan. Here I purposely undercook the scallops, then allow them to poach in the veggie mix toward the end.

Now the third thing: SIZE. Size matters. Since this is all going together, if the smallest ingredient is the corn, the largest thing should be no larger than a quarter. (That's why the scallops are cut in half.) About 99 percent of all cooking issues could be solved by thinking about relative size. If you have a mix of ingredients all cooking together, obviously the larger ingredients are going to take more time. You can address this by allowing them to cook longer in the pan or by ensuring as much uniformity as possible.

Remove the abductor muscle (side muscle) of the scallops and cut each in half top to bottom into half-moons.

In a small bowl, toss the scallops with the dry rub until well coated and season with salt.

In a large heavy-bottomed skillet, heat the oil over medium-high heat until shimmering. Add the scallops and sear until well browned on one side, about 2 minutes. Once seared, shake the pan, rolling the scallops around for a few seconds. Remove the scallops to a plate and set aside.

Add the corn to the same skillet with a splash of oil and cook, stirring occasionally, until charred, about 4 minutes. (You may want to put a lid on the pan, since the kernels can pop like crazy.) Once tender, transfer the corn to a plate.

Add another splash of oil to the same pan, add the mushrooms, and cook until golden brown and tender, 4 to 6 minutes. Don't agitate the pan too much or the mushrooms won't brown. Once browned, transfer to the plate with the corn and set aside.

Add another splash of oil to the same pan, then add the banana peppers and cook for 2 to 3 minutes, allowing them to develop some color.

Finally, add the tomatoes, edamame, butter, sour cream, and tarragon to the pan. Return the corn and mushrooms to the pan, season everything with a big pinch of salt, and stir to combine. Add ½ cup water and bring to a simmer. Cook until the sauce is thick enough to coat the back of a spoon, about 10 minutes.

Add the reserved scallops, allowing to warm for 1 to 2 minutes, until cooked through. Adjust seasoning if necessary. Serve in a large platter or bowl.

CARBS

Very Easy Bread

Makes one 9 by 5-inch loaf • Prep time: 25 minutes • Cook time: 1 hour • Inactive time: 2½ hours

Tangzhong
- 3 tablespoons whole milk
- 2 tablespoons bleached white bread flour

Dough
- 4 tablespoons (2 ounces) unsalted butter, melted, plus more melted for the bowl and pan
- 2½ cups unbleached bread flour, plus more for shaping
- ¼ cup sugar
- 2 tablespoons powdered milk or nonfat dry milk powder
- 2¼ teaspoons instant yeast
- 1¼ teaspoons kosher salt
- ½ cup whole milk, warm (110°F), plus 1 tablespoon cold or room temp
- 1 large egg

Remember when everyone made sourdough and named their starters and took care of them like they were children or plants? I love sourdough as much as anyone, but the whole thing takes more forethought and preparation than I'm capable of. But this bread, this very easy bread, can be made with nothing more than what you have in the pantry and at a moment's notice. The base of it is a milky flour paste called *tangzhong* in Chinese and *yu-dane* in Japanese, which gives steamed buns and milk bread, respectively, their spongy springiness. The result is the sort of pillowy soft bread that, as a Midwesterner, is more my speed than an austere sourdough.

Oh, and look, it calls for dry milk or nonfat dry milk powder. So order those ahead of time.

Make the tangzhong: In a small saucepan, combine the milk, flour, and 3 tablespoons water and whisk until smooth. Place the saucepan over low heat, whisking constantly, until the mixture thickens to the consistency of paste or loose mashed potatoes and you can see the bottom of the pan, 5 to 6 minutes. Transfer the mixture to a small bowl and let cool.

Make the dough: Brush a large bowl and a 9 by 5-inch loaf pan with butter. Set both aside.

In a stand mixer bowl, combine the flour, sugar, powdered milk, yeast, and salt. In a separate bowl, whisk together the warm milk, the egg, the 4 tablespoons melted butter, and the tangzhong. Scrape the liquid ingredients into the stand mixer bowl and mix with a fork for a few seconds just to bring together. Snap on the dough hook, turn the mixer to low speed, and mix until a smooth ball forms (it shouldn't be sticky anymore), roughly 15 minutes.

Transfer the dough to the greased bowl, cover with plastic wrap, and let rest in a warm, draft-free area until almost doubled in size, about 1½ hours.

Gently punch the dough to deflate and turn out onto a lightly floured surface. Roll the dough over itself to form into a log shape, slightly smaller than the size of the loaf pan. Place the log, seam-side down, in the greased loaf pan. (Alternatively, divide the dough into 8 equal portions, about 2 ounces each, and roll into smooth, compact balls and layer the balls of dough into the loaf pan.) Cover the loaf loosely with plastic wrap and allow it to rest until the dough is puffed about 2 inches over the rim of the pan, about 1 hour.

Meanwhile, preheat the oven to 350°F.

Uncover the loaf and brush with the 1 tablespoon milk. Bake until the bread is golden brown on top and a digital thermometer inserted at the center reads 200°F, 30 to 35 minutes, rotating the pan halfway through.

Let the bread cool for 10 minutes in the pan. Invert the loaf onto a wire rack and let cool at least 20 more minutes more before slicing.

Variation

Reese's Pieces Bread: This bread does well with Reese's Pieces and chocolate chips folded into it, though, to be honest, what isn't better with Reese's Pieces and chocolate chips folded into it? When the dough is still in the mixer bowl, add 1 cup semisweet chocolate chips and 1 cup peanut butter chips at the last 5 minutes of mixing.

Relationship Potatoes

Serves 2 • Prep time: 5 minutes • Cook time: 15 minutes

1¼ pounds potatoes (3 Yukon Gold or 2 russets)
Kosher salt
2 tablespoons neutral oil
2 tablespoons unsalted butter
3 garlic cloves, crushed, but skin-on
A few sprigs of fresh thyme
2 teaspoons PX Spice (page 19) or black pepper as needed)

Some recipes you make only in a relationship. These home fries are one of them. When I'm alone, I just have black coffee for breakfast. But this dish is great if you're with someone and it's a day off. After you've cleaned the apartment, you make eggs with homemade hot sauce, and bacon, and these potatoes and then make love all day. Sometimes I think relationships are like home fries: They really work only if the potatoes maintain their own individual forms and don't become a codependent mush. What about boundaries? What about personal space? What about the deep-seated fear of being seen by another person (and the simultaneous deep desire to be seen by another person)? That's why I live alone and why I purposely undercook the potatoes which, ironically, I'll never make as long as I live alone.

Wash the potatoes and quarter them lengthwise, then cut each quarter crosswise into ¼-inch-thick slices.

Place the cut potatoes in a pot with cold water and let them soak for a minute. Add a heavy pinch of salt to the pot and bring it to a boil over medium-high heat. Once the potatoes come to a boil, drain well.

In a large sauté pan, heat the oil and butter over medium heat. Add the drained potatoes to the pan (they should fit in a relatively even layer) and increase the heat to high. Cook undisturbed, until golden brown, about 10 minutes.

Reduce the heat to medium and add the garlic cloves (in their skin) and the thyme sprigs to the pan. Season the potatoes with the PX Spice, and salt and pepper to taste. Cook, stirring, until the potatoes are crispy and just tender, about 2 minutes. Remove the garlic and their skins and reseason the potatoes as needed before serving.

Goddamn American Potatoes Dauphinoise

Serves 4 to 6 • Prep time: 25 minutes • Cook time: 1 hour 10 minutes

- Softened unsalted butter, for the pan
- 2 cups heavy cream
- 3 garlic cloves, grated on a Microplane
- 1 bunch thyme, leaves picked
- Kosher salt and freshly ground black pepper
- 2 pounds Yukon Gold potatoes (6 to 8 medium)
- ¼ cup whole milk
- 8 ounces cheese (Cheddar, Parmesan, or Gruyère), freshly grated (see Notes) (about 2 cups)
- 1 tablespoon chopped fresh parsley
- 1 tablespoon chopped fresh chives

Notes

- It's better to grate your own cheese. Not because you're a snob, but because pregrated cheese is often tossed with cornstarch or potato starch so it doesn't melt the same way.
- Traditionally for this dish you would add milk to the béchamel so it doesn't burn. Here, since you don't have a béchamel in the first place, it's just a nod to my old boss Galliffet.

When I was interning with Jean-Jacques Galliffet at L'Auberge de la Valloir in Épinouze, France, I was not allowed to touch or make anything. I was, however, allowed, and in fact required, to peel mountains of potatoes and slice them thinly for Galliffet's Dauphinoise, a gratin of sliced potatoes baked in cream. Upon receiving this assignment, I gathered everything and a big block of cheese and headed to the prep kitchen. Galliffet approached me, eyeing the cheese with distrust. "What is that for?" "Dauphinoise, chef." "You goddamn Americans with your goddamn cheese. There is no cheese in Dauphinoise!" Galliffet was right, but, I'm an American and cheese is delicious. This version uses a lot of it. (Technically, it's a hybrid of Dauphinoise and a gratin.) Traditionally, you'd make a béchamel to accompany this dish, but you don't even have to—it's still delicious without.

Preheat the oven to 350°F. Generously butter a 9-inch round baking pan. Set aside.

In a small saucepan, combine the cream, garlic, and thyme and bring to a boil over medium heat. Season generously with salt and pepper. Remove from the heat and let the mixture sit while you slice the potatoes.

Peel and thinly slice the potatoes on a mandoline, about 1⁄16 inch thick. Shingle the potatoes into the buttered baking pan in a single layer. Repeat layering until you've used up all the potatoes. Strain the cream mixture over the potatoes. It should almost cover the potatoes but not quite. Top with the milk (see Notes), then evenly sprinkle with the cheese.

Tightly wrap the pan in aluminum foil and bake until you feel very little resistance as you cut through the potatoes, 45 to 50 minutes.

Increase the oven temperature to 400°F, remove the foil, and bake until the top is browned in places, 15 to 20 minutes.

Let sit for 15 minutes before serving, garnished with the parsley and chives.

Giant Latkes

Serves 4 • Prep time: 10 minutes • Cook time: 30 minutes

2 large eggs
¼ cup all-purpose flour
1 teaspoon kosher salt, plus more as needed
½ teaspoon freshly ground black pepper
3 large Yukon Gold potatoes (1 pound 5 ounces), julienned (see Notes)
1 medium yellow onion, thinly sliced
2 tablespoons unsalted butter
2 tablespoons extra-virgin olive oil
1 cup lemon crème fraîche (see Notes)
3 tablespoons chopped fresh chives
Trout roe, whatever you can afford

Notes

- Julienning is a pain in the butt. If you don't want the hassle, use either a box grater or the medium-teeth on a mandoline.
- Lemon crème fraîche is just crème fraîche into which I've added about a lemon's worth of zest. If you have some of those Preserved Lemons (page 31), fold in like a tablespoon per cup.

This is a latke recipe for brunches. I serve it with crème fraîche, chives, and, if I'm feeling fancy, caviar. Cut the latke into wedges and use it like a build-your-own-pizza station. The recipe contains in it a few useful lessons that extend beyond delicious crispy potato pancakes:

1. Messing around with size makes things seem fancy. This is a giant latke, but I've made miniature taquitos and quesadillas in the past. There's nothing special about them except the scale. Making things bigger has the added benefit that in the time it took you to make one, you can feed four people.

2. When making latkes like this or regular hash browns, the trick is to act quickly—as Thomas Keller would say, "with a sense of urgency"—once you salt the potatoes. The salt will draw moisture out from the potatoes, so if you let it sit too long, the entire mixture gets soggy. (Drain the extra moisture if this is the case.)

3. At the end, you'll have 10 minutes for the latkes to be in the oven. That's when you make your eggs or anything else you want. This is a good example of the old adage: Work the stove; don't let the stove work you.

Preheat the oven to 350°F.

In a large bowl, whisk together the eggs, flour, salt, and pepper. Stir in the potatoes and onion to combine.

To make 2 giant latkes: In a 6-inch nonstick sauté pan, heat 1 tablespoon each butter and olive oil over medium heat until fully melted. Scoop half the potato mixture into the pan, pressing down to flatten into an even round all the way to the edges, and sauté until golden brown, 4 to 5 minutes. Place a large plate or sheet pan over the sauté pan and carefully flip the pancake to invert, then slide it back into the pan, browned-side up. Cook until golden brown on the second side, another 4 to 5 minutes. Remove and place on a sheet pan. Repeat with the remaining butter, oil, and potato mixture.

Bake in the oven for 10 minutes. Immediately season with more salt and serve hot, topped with the lemon crème fraîche, chives, and trout roe.

To make 4 large latkes: In a nonstick medium sauté pan, heat ½ tablespoon each of the butter and olive oil over medium heat until fully melted.

Divide the potato mixture into 4 equal piles. Scoop the first into the pan, pressing down to flatten into an even round and sauté, flipping once, until golden brown on both sides, about 3 minutes per side. Remove and place on a sheet pan. Repeat with the remaining butter, oil, and potato mixture until all the latkes have been sautéed.

Bake in the oven for 10 minutes. Immediately season with more salt.

Serve hot, topped with the lemon crème fraîche, chives, and trout roe.

Just a Basic Spaetzle . . . with a Bunch of Variations

Serves 4 • Prep time: 20 minutes • Cook time: 20 minutes

Basic Spaetzle
2 large eggs
½ cup whole milk
1¼ cups all-purpose flour
Kosher salt
Extra-virgin olive oil

To Finish (Optional)
Extra-virgin olive oil
Unsalted butter
Chopped fresh parsley and chives

The reason this dish is so fun and easy to make is because it has only three ingredients: eggs, flour, and milk. Four if you count salt. Everyone pretty much has these at all times, so you can usually make enough spaetzle with whatever you have around. The next part—actually making the spaetzle—you have to MacGyver, unless you have a spaetzle maker, which you probably don't. Some people can do this by spreading the dough in a thin layer on a cutting board and cutting it directly into a pot of boiling water. That's called *handgeschabt Spaetzle*. But if you can do that, you obviously don't need this recipe.

For everyone else, you really just need something to evenly drip the dough into a pot of boiling water. You can use a potato masher (aka a ricer) or you can force the spaetzle dough through a colander or one of those pasta-draining inserts so many stockpots come with. You want your spaetzle to be no smaller than the size of a #2 pencil's eraser.

If doing this over a pot of boiling water seems stressful, after the water comes to a boil, take it off the heat and add the spaetzle in batches, using about a cup of dough at a time. Put the water back on the heat and let it come back to a boil. Once the spaetzle float to the top, scoop them out with a basket strainer or a slotted spoon and set them aside. Once cooked, you can use the spaetzle as you would with any noodle. Like, pasta marinara but with spaetzle. Or make it into a casserole by tossing the spaetzle with chicken, broccoli, and a can of cream of mushroom soup. Broil the thing for 10 minutes until golden brown. But what follows the basic spaetzle are two super-easy flavor variations, and then two recipes that use the cooked spaetzle, whichever flavor you choose.

In a medium bowl, whisk together the eggs and milk until incorporated. In another bowl, sift together the flour and 1 teaspoon kosher salt. Pour the liquid mixture into the flour mixture, while mixing, until a gummy cake batter–like texture is achieved. (Ideally, the batter would sit for 24 hours, covered and refrigerated, to let the flour hydrate, which allows the dough to form more gluten. But, it doesn't really matter. Fuck it. We'll do it live.)

Bring a large pot of salted water to a boil.

Once ready to form the spaetzle, grab a perforated pan like a pasta-draining or steamer insert, if you have one, or a colander with holes the size of a #2 pencil eraser. Pour the batter into the pan, steamer, or colander and push it through the holes with a spatula into the boiling water. Be careful not to crowd the spaetzle, lest they stick together.

Once the spaetzle float to the top, after about 2 minutes or so, allow to simmer for an additional minute. Remove the spaetzle with a slotted spoon into a bowl. Toss with some olive oil, so they don't stick together.

At this point your spaetzle is ready to get dressed. You have some options:

To crisp it

In a sauté pan, heat 1 tablespoon olive oil and 1 tablespoon butter over medium heat. Once the butter is foamy, add the spaetzle. Don't shake it too often, perhaps every minute. As the spaetzle crisps, it'll soufflé (it is, after all, just flour and egg). Once it is GBD (golden brown and delicious), finish with some chopped parsley and chives and serve.

To treat it like a buttered noodle

Make a beurre monté (emulsified butter sauce) by heating 2 tablespoons water in a small sauté pan over medium heat until it comes to a boil. Add 8 tablespoons butter, 1 tablespoon at a time, adding each as soon as the previous tablespoon is almost completely melted and constantly swirling. As soon as the butter is melted, remove from the heat and toss with the spaetzle and some chopped parsley and chives. Serve immediately.

Variations

- **Mustard Spaetzle:** Add ½ cup Dijon mustard to the batter when mixing it.
- **Pea Spaetzle:** Microwave 1 cup frozen peas and 1 cup spinach or kale for 3 minutes on high. Transfer to a food processor and blend to a puree. Add the batter to the food processor and blend again for 1 minute.

made-in
made-in

made·in
made·in

SPAETZLE STROGANOFF

Serves 4

Just a Basic Spaetzle or Variation (page 186 or 187)
1 tablespoon extra-virgin olive oil
1 tablespoon unsalted butter
8 ounces button mushrooms, cleaned and quartered
1 small onion, thinly sliced (about 1 cup)
Kosher salt and freshly ground black pepper
1 tablespoon all-purpose flour
2 cups chicken stock or water
2 tablespoons Dijon mustard
½ cup sour cream
Dash of red wine vinegar
¼ cup finely chopped fresh dill
¼ cup finely chopped fresh parsley

Make and boil the spaetzle as directed.

In a large sauté pan, heat the olive oil and butter over medium heat. Once the butter is foaming, add the mushrooms and onion together, seasoning with a dash of salt and pepper. Cover the pan and cook down for 5 minutes. Uncover and stir in the flour, forming a roux with the mushroomy water and fat. Once a roux forms, deglaze the pan with the stock, making sure to scrape up any browned bits, and bring to a boil.

Once boiling, add the spaetzle, let it return to a boil, then reduce the heat to medium-low and simmer for about 5 minutes, or until the spaetzle is hot. Add the mustard, sour cream, and vinegar and reduce the heat to low. Season with salt and pepper again. Allow the sauce to reduce for an additional 15 minutes, then check for seasoning again and stir in the dill and parsley, reserving a pinch to top at the very end.

MAC AND CHEESE SPAETZLE

Serves 4

Just a Basic Spaetzle or Variation (page 186 or 187)
3 tablespoons unsalted butter
3 tablespoons all-purpose flour
2 cups whole milk
1½ cups shredded Cheddar cheese
1 tablespoon yellow mustard
1 teaspoon onion powder
Dash of hot sauce
½ cup bread crumbs
¼ cup finely chopped fresh parsley
Kosher salt and freshly ground pepper

Make and boil the spaetzle as directed.

In a saucepan, melt the butter over medium-low heat. Once melted, add the flour and cook for 5 minutes, stirring constantly. Slowly pour in the milk, whisking as you do, and bring to a boil. Reduce the heat to low and simmer for 5 minutes.

Remove from the heat and add the Cheddar, mustard, onion powder, and the dash of hot sauce, whisking until the cheese has melted.

Add the spaetzle to a large bowl and combine with three-quarters of the sauce (see note at left).

In a separate bowl, mix together the bread crumbs, parsley, and salt and pepper to taste.

Spoon into individual dishes and sprinkle with the bread crumb mixture.

ALWAYS KEEP A LITTLE SAUCE BACK SO YOU CAN ADJUST TO YOUR PREFERENCE. AS THE CHEESE SAUCE THICKENS, YOU MIGHT END UP WANTING TO ADD TO THE REST. OR IF YOU DON'T NEED ALL THE SAUCE, RESERVE IT FOR ANOTHER DISH LIKE NACHOS.

Sweet Potato and Leek Pierogies

Makes 24 pierogies • Prep time: 50 minutes • Cook time: 25 minutes • Inactive time: 1 hour

Dough
2 cups tipo "00" flour, plus more for rolling
1 cup sour cream
1 tablespoon kosher salt

Filling
2 sweet potatoes (1½ pounds total)
1 leek (14 ounces), dark green tops trimmed off
4 tablespoons (2 ounces) unsalted butter
Kosher salt and freshly ground black pepper

To Finish
Kosher salt
Beurre monté (see page 187), for serving
1 lemon, cut into wedges
¼ cup minced fresh chives, for garnish
¼ cup Red Cabbage Sauerkraut (page 33)

One of the big myths about restaurants is that all the dishes (and all the menus) flow directly and solely from the chef. Not so. Many do, but the cooks you hire have an enormous influence on the menu—and in my case, on how I eat at home. This pierogi recipe came from a cook who was at Olmsted for a year—a Canadian guy who wanted to improve his New York City fine-dining chops. He really wanted to show me his pierogi recipe and, well, I love a good dumpling, so . . .

Though many people have dedicated their lives to making pasta, I have not. So I have a couple of back-pocket recipes that I always turn to: a basic spaetzle (see page 186) and this recipe for pierogi. Both are incredibly versatile. Here I'm giving you a sweet potato and leek filling, but experiment with your own fillings. Try ricotta, mushrooms, duck confit. My feelings won't be hurt.

Make the dough: In a food processor, combine the flour, sour cream, and salt and blend until a dough comes together, about 1 minute.

Turn out the dough onto a sheet of plastic wrap and form into a disk. Refrigerate until cold, at least 1 hour.

Make the filling: Prick the sweet potatoes all over with the tines of a fork and microwave for 8 to 10 minutes, flipping halfway through, until tender. Let cool slightly, then peel and place the flesh into a bowl. Mash with a fork until smooth.

Meanwhile, halve the white and light-green part of the leek lengthwise, thinly slice, and wash thoroughly.

In a small sauté pan, melt the butter over medium heat. Add the leek and season with salt and pepper. Cook, stirring occasionally, until softened, 3 to 4 minutes. Add to the mashed sweet potato and mix to combine. Season with salt and pepper to taste and let cool.

Dust a few sheet pans with flour and set aside.

Divide the dough into 8 equal portions. Transfer one piece of dough to a well-floured surface and flatten slightly.

Dust a pasta machine (see Note, page 194) with flour and pat each side of the dough generously with flour. Beginning with the widest number (1) and gradually working your way to the thinnest (7), feed the dough through the pasta maker. Lay down flat on a floured sheet pan and loosely cover. If your dough is tearing, pat it with more flour, fold the sheet in half, and feed it through the machine again. Repeat with the rest of the dough, making sure to keep the finished sheets covered so they don't dry out.

Dust a pierogi tray (see Note, page 194) with flour and lay a sheet of dough over the tray. Gently press the top piece of the pierogi maker into the dough to make divots and remove. Into each divot, place 1 tablespoon of the filling. Top with another pasta sheet. Using a rolling pin, roll over the top of the pierogi tray to cut and seal the dough. The finished pierogies will drop from the bottom. Repeat with the remaining dough and filling to make 24 pierogies.

To finish: Bring a large pot of salted water to a boil over medium-high heat. Working in batches, add the pierogies and cook until they float, 1 to 2 minutes. Drain.

Continued

Sweet Potato and Leek Pierogies, Continued

From here, toss in the beurre monté and serve with the lemon, chives, and sauerkraut.

Or pat the pierogies dry and fry them in oil for about 2 minutes a side until crisp.

Store cooked pierogies in the refrigerator for up to 5 days or in the freezer for up to 3 months. If freezing, you can store either cooked or uncooked pierogies. Simply freeze on a cookie sheet so they're not touching, and once they're frozen, place in zip-seal plastic bags. If freezing after the pierogies are cooked, just pat them dry before freezing.

Note: If you don't already have a pasta maker or pasta sheeter, you can get a stand-alone pasta machine for about $30, or if you have a KitchenAid anyway, a pasta sheeting attachment for about $40. And you will also need a pierogi tray (I mean, it's a recipe for pierogies). They're available on Amazon and cost about $20. I live in a small apartment and hate buying things, but I did get myself a pierogi maker.

FUCK IT, INSTANT MASHED POTATO PIEROGIES: MAKE THE DOUGH AND FILL THE PIEROGIES WITH INSTANT MASHED POTATOES. JUST FOLLOW THE PACKAGE DIRECTIONS.

A PECK OF PICKLED PEPPERS PIEROGIES

Serves 3 to 4 • Prep time: 10 minutes • Cook time: 5 minutes • Inactive time: 1 hour

3 small multicolored peppers (2½ ounces), sliced
½ cup red wine vinegar or distilled white vinegar
Kernels from 1 ear of corn (14 ounces)
4 tablespoons (2 ounces) unsalted butter
12 pierogies, boiled
1 cup halved mixed cherry tomatoes (4 ounces)
2 tablespoons minced fresh chives

In a small bowl, toss the peppers with the red wine vinegar and let sit for at least 1 hour or at most the day.

In a small microwave-safe bowl, microwave the corn on high for about 2 minutes, or until tender.

In a large sauté pan, heat 2 tablespoons water over medium heat until it boils. Add the butter, 1 tablespoon at a time, adding each as soon as the previous tablespoon is almost completely melted and constantly swirling.

As soon as the butter is melted, add the pierogies, corn, drained pickled peppers, and tomatoes and cook, tossing together, until warmed through, 1 to 2 minutes.

Serve topped with the chives.

SWEET THINGS

Old-School Chocolate Mousse, Two Ways

Serves 8 • Prep time: 25 minutes • Cook time: 10 minutes • Inactive time: 3 hours

2 cups dark chocolate chips (72% cacao)
2 tablespoons unsalted butter
6 eggs, separated
4 tablespoons sugar
⅛ teaspoon salt
⅛ teaspoon cream of tartar
Crème fraîche or (or *and!*) whipped cream, for serving (optional)

What makes this chocolate mousse old school is the eggs. They're raw. OMG, I know, right? But get over it. This is how Escoffier intended the recipe when he developed it in the nineteenth century. (Most contemporary mousses are made with whipped cream, gelatin, and chocolate.) But a mousse should have eggs in it. That's what makes a mousse, not a pudding. This was a lesson I first learned while staging at the Auberge de la Valloire in Épinouze, France, in 2002. I worked for three months, living in the maid's quarters, and came home with this rich, silky, eggy chocolate mousse, a potatoes Dauphinoise recipe (see page 182), and a bad case of mono. I treasure two of those three things. Mousse suffers from the reputation of being difficult to make, whereas actually it's one of the easiest desserts to throw together. Ever wonder why so many restaurants have a chocolate mousse on the dessert menu? Often it's because there's no pastry chef, and you need no pastry skills to make this delectable dessert. And as an extra bonus, when you freeze mousse, it becomes a marquise, which sounds even fancier. Classic twofer.

In a small saucepan, melt together the chocolate and butter over medium heat. (You just want it to be melted, not overly hot.) Remove from the heat.

In a stand mixer fitted with the whisk, whisk together the egg yolks and 2 tablespoons of the sugar until ribbons form. Remove to a separate large bowl and set aside.

Wash and dry the bowl and whisk attachment of your stand mixer thoroughly. In the bowl, combine the egg whites, salt, and cream of tartar. Whisk until they become frothy (almost the consistency of a whipped cream), then add the remaining sugar. Continue whipping until the whites form soft peaks.

Pour the chocolate/butter mixture into the bowl with the egg yolk/sugar mixture, stirring until incorporated. Then, in thirds, fold in the whipped egg whites until completely incorporated, but careful not to overmix (don't freak out!).

For old-school mousse

Portion one half of the mousse into four serving dishes or a bowl, cover, and refrigerate for at least 3 hours until set.

When ready to serve the mousse, remove from the fridge and let sit at room temperature for 30 minutes. Serve with crème fraîche or whipped cream, if using.

For the marquise

Portion the other half of the mousse into a plastic-lined loaf pan and freeze. Frozen mousse is called a marquise. Cool, right?

When ready to serve the marquise, let it sit out for 10 minutes, then pop it out of the loaf pan, slice like a cake, and serve frozen, topped with crème fraîche and whipped cream, if using.

Sad Cookie for One

Makes 1 cookie • Prep time: 5 minutes • Cook time: 20 minutes

- 1 tablespoon unsalted butter, at room temperature
- 1 tablespoon light brown sugar
- 1 teaspoon granulated sugar
- 1 teaspoon beaten egg yolk
- ¼ teaspoon pure vanilla extract
- 2 tablespoons all-purpose flour
- ¼ teaspoon baking soda
- ⅛ teaspoon kosher salt
- 1 tablespoon dark chocolate chips, plus a few more for the top

Every evening after dinner, as I'm sitting on my couch, I get a hankering for something sweet. Often, I have bodega ice cream sandwiches in the freezer. Sometimes I don't. For those times, I have to make a cookie. It takes the same amount of time to make 1 cookie as it does 24 cookies, but if I made 24 cookies, I'd eat 24 cookies. So this recipe makes just one solitary cookie for one solitary cookie monster.

Preheat the oven to 350°F. Line a baking sheet with parchment paper.

In a small bowl, combine the butter, light brown sugar, granulated sugar, the egg yolk, and vanilla and stir until smooth and creamy. Stir in the flour, baking soda, and salt and mix until fully combined. Stir in the chocolate chips. Form the dough into a smooth ball and place on the lined baking sheet. Top with a few more chocolate chips. Freeze for 10 minutes.

Bake until browned and set around the edges (it should still look a little gooey in the center), 15 to 18 minutes. Let cool slightly on the pan before eating.

Honey Butterscotch

Yield: about 1 pint • Prep time: 15 mins • Cook time: 10 minutes

- 4 tablespoons (2 ounces) unsalted butter
- ½ cup packed dark brown sugar
- ½ cup heavy cream
- 1 teaspoon kosher salt
- 1 teaspoon vanilla extract
- ¼ cup honey

Back when I worked at Alinea, we used (a more complicated version of) this recipe to make a butterscotch that we'd fashion into ribbons and wrap around dehydrated bacon, which we'd then hang from a wire so it looked like delicious ham laundry. Now I use it to pour over ice cream I get from Van Leeuwen, the ice cream shop down the street from me, when I'm tired but want something sweet. Seasons of life, I guess.

Melt the butter in a saucepot on low heat. Add the brown sugar and stir until melted. Add the cream, salt, and vanilla and bring to a boil. Reduce the heat and simmer for 5 minutes. Add the honey and simmer for another 3 minutes. Let cool slightly (it will thicken as it sits) before serving over Van Leeuwen vanilla ice cream.

Entenmann's Chocolate Cake

Serves 1 person • Prep time: 5 minutes • Cook time: n/a

1 Entenmann's Chocolate Fudge Iced Cake

Sometimes, I have to admit, even the prospect of turning on the oven or stove is too daunting for me. That's okay. You'd be amazed by what chefs eat on their off-hours. I don't mean the mouthwatering recipes from their _______ *at Home* cookbooks. I mean, like, for real . . . when they come home at midnight or later, exhausted and starving. Would I ever serve a highly processed superfood like a shelf-stable chocolate cake at any of my restaurants? No. But when it's 1 o'clock in the morning, I'm all amped up after service, and I need to unwind, is there anything better to eat while watching *Malcolm in the Middle*? Absolutely not.

Go to a bodega on the way home. Place the cake on the counter and pay. Combine the cake and the receipt in a plastic bag and transport home.

Once home, remove the cake from the bag and then from the container. Place on a plate and carry to the couch. To serve, eat while lightly dusting chin, hands, shirt, and pants with cake crumbs.

Entenmann's
Pop'Ettes
NET WT 14 OZ (397g)
Entenmann's
CHOCOLATE FUDGE ICED CAKE
330 CALORIES
UNIT PRICE PER LB
Entenmann's
CHOCOLATE FUDGE ICED CAKE
NET WT 1 LB 3 OZ (539g)
8 CRUMB TOPPED DONUTS
MINI BROWNIE CAKES
CHOCOLATE CHIP
8 INDIVIDUALLY WRAPPED CAKES
Entenmann's
Baker's Delights
8 INDIVIDUALLY WRAPPED CAKES
EASY OPEN ZIPPER
PULL HERE
MINI BROWNIE CAKES CHOCOLATE CHIP
Entenmann's CLASSIC
8 CRUMB TOPPED DONUTS

DRINKS

Pickled Raspberry Shrub

Serves 4 • Prep Time: 10 minutes • Cook time: n/a

2 tablespoons Pickled Raspberries (page 39, see Note)
1 tablespoon fresh lime juice
Ginger beer
Ice
1 lime wedge, for garnish

Note: Make sure to use fresh pickled raspberries for this recipe, as those that have been stored with olive oil won't be terribly appetizing.

I generally don't like mocktails. We're sober, not sweet-toothed. But this one has no added sugar, except that which was used in the pickling liquid for the raspberries. It's refreshing and a little tart like a shrub—or drinking vinegar—should be.

Stir together the raspberries and lime juice. Add the ginger beer to top up the drink and gently stir. Serve over ice, garnished with a slice of lime.

Lemon Basil Shandy

Serves 4 • Prep time: 5 minutes • Cook time: 5 minutes

- ½ cup sugar
- 2 tablespoons grated lemon zest (from 2 lemons)
- 1 sprig basil, crushed between your palms, plus 1 ploosh fresh basil, for garnish
- 1 cup fresh lemon juice (5 lemons)
- Three 12-ounce cans Athletic Brewing Upside Dawn, chilled
- Two 12-ounce cans sparkling water, chilled

Look, just because I can't drink beer—because if do I'll likely end up passed out, blacked out, or back at rehab—doesn't mean I don't love the taste. Thankfully, since I got sober, a range of very good nonalcoholic beers have hit the market. Among them is Athletic Brewing. Clean, balanced, light-bodied, and gluten-free (not that I care), their Upside Dawn is a perfect beer for a shandy, a cocktail usually made with beer and citrus.

In a small saucepan, combine the sugar and 1 cup water and bring to a boil, stirring to dissolve the sugar. Remove from the heat and stir in the lemon zest and basil. Let cool completely, about 20 minutes.

Stir in the lemon juice. Strain (you should have about 2 cups). Transfer the lemon syrup to the fridge until well chilled.

To serve, divide the lemon syrup among 4 pint glasses. Fill each glass three-quarters of the way full with beer and top with sparkling water. Garnish with some basil leaves.

Variation

Lemon Basil Shandy over Ice: Personally, I like this served over ice. If you do use ice, cut the lemon base in half—that is, 1 tablespoon zest and ½ cup juice—since you'll have less room in the glass, but keep the rest of the ratios: ⅓ lemon syrup, ⅓ beer, ⅓ sparkling water.

Thai-ish NA Bloody Mary

Makes 2 drinks • Prep time: 5 minutes • Cook time: 5 minutes • Inactive time: At least 2 hours

¼ cup packed palm sugar or brown sugar
3 lime leaves
1 tablespoon fresh lime juice
¼ cup fresh basil
½ Fresno chile, sliced
½ cup Tomato Water (recipe follows; see note below)
Ice
Chilled sparkling water, for serving
Lime wheels, for serving

Clarifying juices—turning them clear—is a neat method you'll see in fancy restaurants, something vaguely modernist but still approachable. There are a few techniques for doing this. Some involve freezing the juice with agar-agar, a product derived from algae. Or you can blitz the ingredient to be juiced and then strain it through a cheesecloth. I prefer the latter method because there's little work and little waste. This vaguely Thai Bloody Mary is elevated by the clarified tomato water, which is also a great way to use up bruised or soft tomatoes. While heirloom tomatoes can cost $6 or $7 at the farmers' market, you can get a bag of soft tomatoes for a buck.

In a small saucepan, combine the palm sugar and ¼ cup water over medium heat, stirring until the sugar dissolves. Remove from the heat and add the lime leaves, lime juice, basil, chile, and Tomato Water. Let cool.

Add about ¼ cup of the mix to each glass. Add ice, top with a couple splashes of sparkling water, garnish with lime wheels, if desired, and serve.

TOMATO WATER

Makes 1¼ cups

1 pound overripe tomatoes, torn or roughly chopped

In a food processor, blend the tomatoes until smooth. Line a sieve with a few layers of cheesecloth and set over a large bowl. Pour the tomato puree into the sieve and tie up the ends over the puree, forming a pouch. Let stand at room temperature for at least 2 hours (you can also leave it in the refrigerator overnight and just let it do its thing). The tomato water will drip out and separate from the pulp. It will be tomatoey but refreshing. Save the leftover pulp for tomato sauce.

IF YOU DON'T WANT TO BOTHER WITH CLARIFYING TOMATO WATER, JUST USE PLAIN OLD TOMATO JUICE. IT WON'T BE AS CLEAR BUT IT WILL BE EQUALLY DELICIOUS.

Uses

- Add a couple leaves of basil and a pinch of salt, warm it up in a pot, and serve it with fish. Call it a tomato consommé.
- Combine with some olive oil. Season with salt and pour over a crudo.

Acknowledgments

FROM GREG BAXTROM

Thank you from the bottom of my heart to all staff members past and present for their immense talents and skills. From dishwasher to general manager, you make everything possible. A special thank-you to Jenny Treantafilos, Kyle Bentley, Taylor Hester, Morgan Schofield, Ben Davis, Fernando Dinen, Daruby Pena, Yuberkis Santana, and Sherry Cardoso. Your dedication makes the hospitality industry a better place to be.

To Chef Grant Achatz: For nearly twenty years you have been my mentor. I have come to you during my highs and lows. Your belief in me when I was just an inexperienced nineteen-year-old cook has been a driving force in my motivation to keep going.

To Chef John Shields: You taught me everything at Alinea when I was just starting out. You are a great leader, teacher, and someone I look up to deeply.

To Chef Dan Barber: I was immature and we didn't always get along, but I wouldn't be where I am today without the opportunities you gave me and the knowledge I took from you.

To my super-talented chef friends: Corey Chow, Matt Peters, and Travis Swikard for your support.

To Chris Haatuft, my Norwegian brother from another mother. Thank you for always being there, during the highest highs and lowest lows.

To Nick Hirst for being 50 percent friend and 50 percent attorney.

To Azemina: For your endless second chances and seeing there is good in me. I wouldn't be on this earth without you.

To David Posey, for being my go-to friend every time I'm back home in Chicago.

To my brother, Kevin, my father, Mike, and mother, Patti Ann: Thank you for being by my side the entire time and never making me feel like an outsider.

To my sister, Katie: A big thank-you for rising to the challenge and helping get me the help I needed when I was at my worst.

To Suzanne Cupps: Thank you for pushing me to be healthier, explore new things, and to keep going to the farmers' market.

To the team at Mona Creative: Thank you for always helping us get the word out on our efforts and being our #1 supporters, Ilana Alperstein, Eva Karagiorgas, Cassandra Chamoun.

To Jerry and Jessica Seinfeld. Thank you for opening your home and creating such a lovely place to cook and grow.

To Joshua David Stein: Thank you for being someone I felt comfortable opening up to and helping me find my voice. I said that if you helped polish the acknowledgments you could write anything here. Like, thank you for being the most brilliant writer. You can eat for free at all my restaurants forever.

To Riley Wofford: Thank you for testing each and every recipe to make sure they were perfect for this book.

To Murray Hall: Thank you for the wonderful photography.

To David Black: Thank you for pushing me since day one of Olmsted to get this book done.

To Cristina Garces and Molly Birnbaum, editor and publisher at Ten Speed Press: Thank you for having the excitement and wisdom to allow us to make such an exciting book. And thank you to the rest of the Ten Speed team: Lizzie Allen, Jessica Heim, Emily Hotaling, Abby Oladipo, Kristin Sargianis, and Natalie Yera-Campbell.

FROM JOSHUA DAVID STEIN

First of all and most important, thank you, Greg, for allowing me to help tell your story.

Thank you to everyone at Olmsted and Patti Ann's, including former Olmsteders Sherry Cardoso and Samantha Ortiz, for feeding me—physically and emotionally—during this process.

Thank you to everyone who helped make this book possible, a vast and talented team: Riley Wofford for her stellar and punctilious recipe testing, Murray Hall for his wonderful photography, Cristina Garces and Molly Birnbaum from Ten Speed for their sage and thorough editing. Thank you to Kate Slate and Lizzie Allen, for making sure this book is error-free and pretty.

Thank you to David Black and Sarah Smith at the David Black Agency for their advocacy and sage wisdom.

By the time you read this, I will have closed Olmsted and Patti Ann's, my two restaurants in Brooklyn. Only 5 Acres in Rockefeller Center remains open. This was an incredibly tough decision. These restaurants were not just where I spent most of my time but also places I physically built with my father. They truly felt like a second home, and I'm sad to be losing them before I was ready to let them go. While I'm not always the most optimistic person, I feel a sense of optimism now. My neighborhood has provided me with great success, and it's time to branch out and explore new opportunities.

Index

Note: Page references in *italics* indicate photographs.

S

T

V

Y

1745 Broadway
New York, NY 10019
tenspeed.com
penguinrandomhouse.com

Typeface: Weltkern'sTWK Lausanne

Library of Congress Cataloging-in-Publication Data is on file with the publisher.

Hardcover ISBN 978-1-9848-6356-0
Ebook ISBN 978-1-9848-6357-7

Acquiring editor: Molly Birnbaum | Project editor: Cristina Garces | Production editor: Abby Oladipo
Designer and art director: Lizzie Allen | Production designer: Merri Ann Morrell
Production: Jessica Heim
Food stylist: Pearl Jones
Prop stylist: Sophia Eleni Pappas | Prop stylist assistants: Sappho Hocker and Samuel Campoli
Photo assistant: Jonathan Bumble
Copy editor: Kate Slate | Proofreaders: Penelope Haynes, Rachel Holzman, Nancy Inglis, and Robin Slutzky
Indexer: Elizabeth Parson
Publicist: Natalie Yera-Campbell | Marketer: Emily Hotaling

Manufactured in China

10 9 8 7 6 5 4 3 2 1

First Edition

The authorized representative in the EU for product safety and compliance is Penguin Random House Ireland, Morrison Chambers, 32 Nassau Street, Dublin D02 YH68, Ireland, https://eu-contact.penguin.ie.